A GENEALOGIST'S BIBLIOGRAPHY

A Genealogist's Bibliography

Cecil R. Humphery-Smith

GENEALOGICAL PUBLISHING CO., INC.

Baltimore 1985

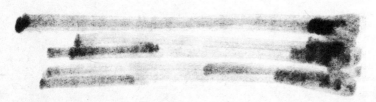

Published in the U.S.A. by
Genealogical Publishing Co., Inc.
Baltimore, Maryland, 1985
© Cecil R. Humphery-Smith, 1985
All Rights Reserved
Library of Congress Catalogue Card Number 85-80388
International Standard Book Number 0-8063-1130-4

Published in Great Britain by
Phillimore & Co., Ltd.
Shopwyke Hall, Chichester, Sussex
1985

Printed and bound in Great Britain

CONTENTS

INTRODUCTION

Since H.G. Harrison's *Select Bibliography of English Genealogy* appeared in 1937 no adequate attempt has been made to produce an updated handbook to replace Gatfield's *Guide* of 90 years ago. Amateur genealogists and local historians have been greatly helped by Mrs. Kaminkov's two small volumes, *A New Bibliography of British Genealogy from Booksellers' Catalogs* and *Genealogical Manuscripts in British Libraries.* The present list does not pretend to replace these. It is based on my interleaved copy of Harrison's work and is intended primarily for students of genealogy and family history.

In this new edition, I hope that I have included those books and publications recommended by my reviewers whom I must thank for their encouragement and enthusiastic comments. I have added a number of other works which have come to my notice for their usefulness within the past five years. Users may also care to know that students at the Institute are assisting in the preparation of a bibliography of guides to sources which have been written up in a wide variety of magazines and journals. My thanks are due to all who have contributed to improving this edition, in particular to Steve Rudd, Manager of the Phillimore Bookshop, and Dr. Frances Condick, of Phillimore's Editorial Department, who have respectively provided many additional entries and overseen the production of the book.

Because of the proliferation of popular books on the subject I have concentrated on those works which will assist students of genealogy before General Registration and national Censuses, and the classic for this period is still Stacey Grimaldi's *Origines Genealogicae* (1837). For the modern period I know I have omitted many good books but have listed a few trustworthy guides which are still available, along with guides to special topics. Any serious student will join the Society of Genealogists, or pursue a course of training through the Institute of Heraldic and Genealogical Studies' School of Family History, and use their libraries. Both have extensive collections.

Considerable help and further bibliographical material are given in the *National Index of Parish Registers*, in Gerald Hamilton-Edwards's books *In Search of Ancestry* and *In Search of Scottish Ancestry*, and in reference library catalogues. Manchester Public Libraries' catalogue is particularly useful.

There is no claim that this guide list is in any way exhaustive. Much more will be found in the pages and footnotes in county histories – in the *Victoria County History* series in particular; in the class catalogues at the British Library; at the libraries of the universities and colleges, as well as more locally, in public, county and diocesan record offices. Whitaker's *Almanac* will provide addresses of record offices and societies with document collections. Jacob's *Law Dictionary* and Burn's *Ecclesiastical Forms* will be treasured guides to those many obscure points which I have neglected to mention in the glossary.

CECIL R. HUMPHERY-SMITH
Canterbury, 1985

Sources: Counties

General

HUMPHREYS, A. L., *A Handbook to County Bibliography; Being a Bibliography of Bibliographies relating to the Counties and Towns of Great Britain and Ireland* (London 1917)

Bedfordshire

Record Repositories and Libraries

Bedfordshire County Record Office, County Hall, Bedford MK42 9AP

Feet of Fines

HUNTER, JOSEPH, (ed.), 'Fines sive pedes finium sive finales concordiae in curia domini regis, ab anno septimo regum regis Ricardi I ad annum decimum sextum regis Johannis 1195 - 1214'. 2 vols. (*Texts and Calendars 33, London Record Commission*, 1835-44). Vol. I covers Beds., Berks., Bucks., Cambs., Cornwall; Vol. II covers Cumberland, Derbyshire, Devon, Dorset.
'Feet of Fines in the Reign of Henry II (and Richard I) 1182 - 1198'. 3 vols. (*Pipe Roll Society Publications* 17, 20, 23, 1894-8).
FOWLER, G. H., (ed.), 'A Calendar of the Feet of Fines for Bedfordshire preserved in the Public Record Office of the reigns of Richard I, John and Henry III' (Parts I and II, *Bedfordshire Historical Record Society* vol. 6, 1919)
FOWLER, G. H., (ed.), 'A Calendar of the Feet of Fines for Bedfordshire ... 1273 - 1307, with supplementary fines from various sources' (Part III, *Bedfordshire Historical Record Society* vol. 12, 1928)

Heraldry

SUMMERS, PETER, (ed.), *Hatchments in Britain, vol. 4: Bucks., Beds., Berks., Wilts.* (1983)

Inquisitiones Post Mortem

FOWLER, G. H., (ed.), 'Calendar of Inquisitiones Post Mortem, 1250-71' (*Bedfordshire Historical Record Society*, vol. 5, 1920)
FOWLER, G. H., (ed.), 'Calendar of Inquisitiones Post Mortem, 1272-86' (*Bedfordshire Historical Record Society*, Vol. 19, 1937)

Parochial and Non-Parochial Registers

BLAYDES, F. A., *Genealogia Bedfordienses: being a collection of evidences relating to the landed gentry of Bedfordshire, 1538-1700, from parish registers etc.* (1890)

Place Names

MAWER, F., and STENTON, F. M., (eds.), *The English Place Names Society, vol 3, Bedfordshire and Huntingdonshire* (1926)

Subsidies

HERVEY, S. H. A., (ed.), *Two Bedfordshire Subsidy Lists, 1309, 1332* (1925)

Visitations

BLAYDES, F. A., (ed.), 'The Visitations of 1565, 1582 and 1634' (*Harleian Society*, vol. 19, 1884)

Wills and Administrations

BELL, PATRICIA, 'Bedfordshire Wills, 1480-1519' (*Bedfordshire Historical Record Society*, vol. 45, 1966)

BLAYDES, F. A., (ed.), *Calendar of some Bedfordshire Wills*, Bedford, Timaeus (1893)

HARVEY, W., *Index to some Bedfordshire Wills* (1888)

NAUGHTON, K. S., *The Gentry of Bedfordshire in the 13th and 14th Centuries* (1976)

Berkshire

Record Repositories and Libraries

Berkshire Record Office, Shire Hall, Shinfield Park, Reading
Reading Corporation, Archives Dept., Central Public Library, Blagrave St.
The Aerary, Dean's Cloister, St George's Chapel, Windsor Castle, Windsor
Eton College Archives, Eton College, Windsor
Sources for Genealogy in the Berkshire Record Office, Berkshire Record Office (1979)

Feet of Fines

see Bedfordshire entry

Heraldry

SPOKES, P. S., 'Coats of arms in Berkshire churches', *Berkshire Archaeological Journal*, 1936
see also Bedfordshire entry

Marriage Registers

Berkshire, Buckinghamshire and Oxfordshire Archaeological Journal, vols. 6-10, 1900-04, contains indexes to marriages in Bradfield, East Ilsley, Purley, Ruscombe, Yattendon.
Phillimore Marriage Registers for Berkshire, 2 vols., 1908, 1914, contain transcripts for Bradfield, Busut, W. Hanney, Hanvell, W. Hundred, Kingston Lisle, Purley, Sparshilt, Sulham, Wantage, W. Woodbay.

Parochial and Non-Parochial Registers

Parish Registers of the Archdeaconry of Berkshire: a Handlist (Berkshire Record Office, 1981)

Pedigrees

BERRY, W., *County Genealogies: Pedigrees of Berkshire families: London, Sherwood, Gilbert and Piper* (1837)

Place Names

STREAT, REV. W. W., *The Place Names of Berkshire*
GELLING, M., (ed.), *The English Place Names Society*, vols. 49, 50, 51, Berkshire parts *I, II, III* (1972, 1973, 1976)

Records of St George's Chapel, Windsor

FELLOWES, E. H., *The Knights of the Garter 1348-1939* (1939)
FELLOWES, E. H., *The Military Knights of Windsor, 1352-1944* (1944)
FELLOWES, E. H., *The Vicars and Minor Canons of His Majesty's Free Chapel of St George in Windsor Castle* (1945)
FELLOWES, E. H., and POYSER, E. R., *The Baptism, Marriage and Burial Registers of St George's Chapel, Windsor Castle* (1957)
HOLMES, Grace, *The Order of the Garter 1348-1984* (1984)
OLLARD, S. L., *Fasti Wyndesorienses: The Deans and Canons of St George's Chapel* (1950)

School Registers

RICHARDSON, W. H., (ed.), *A list of some distinguished persons educated at Abingdon School, Berkshire, 1563-1855* (1905)

Visitations

BARRON, O., (ed.), 'Visitation of 1532', *The Genealogist*, n.s. vol. 14, 1897
METCALFE, W. C., (ed.), 'Visitation of 1566', *The G.*, n. s. vols. 1-2, 1884-5
METCALFE, W. C., (ed.), 'V. of 1665/6', *The G.*, vols. 5-6, 1881-2

Wills and Administrations

COLLIARD, A. N., *List of Berkshire Archdeaconry Registered Wills, 1653-1710, deposited in the Bodleian Library, Oxford* (1960)
HOWSE, J. E., (ed.), 'Berkshire Probate Records 1653-1710' (*British Record Society Index Library*, vol. 87, 1975)
PHILLIMORE, W. P. W., 'Index to Wills ... 1508-1652' (*British Record Society Index Library*, vol. 8, 1893)
'Early Berkshire Wills, pre 1558' (*Berkshire, Buckinghamshire and Oxfordshire Archaeological Journal*, vols. 1, 7, 1895, 1901)
'Berkshire Probate Records 1508-1652' (*British Record Society* vol. 8, 1893 and *Oxford Historical Society*, vol. 23, 1893)
RYLANDS, W. H., (ed.), 'Visitations of 1532, 1566, 1623, 1665/6', *Harleian Society*, vol. 56, 1907

Buckinghamshire

Record Repositories and Libraries

Buckinghamshire County Record Office, County Hall, Aylesbury
Buckinghamshire Archaeological Society, The County Museum, Church St., Aylesbury
Notes for the Guidance of Genealogists (Buckinghamshire County Record Office)

Episcopal Registers and Registers of Clergy

'Wills of Buckinghamshire Clergy in the 16th Century' (*Records of Buckinghamshire*, vol. 13)

Feet of Fines

see Bedfordshire entry above

Heraldry

see Bedfordshire entry above

Pedigrees

BERRY, W., *County Pedigrees: Pedigrees of the Families in the County of Buckinghamshire* (1837)
DE FRAINE, G. M., *Index to the County of Buckingham Poll of 1784 and 1839*

Marriage Bonds

'Buckinghamshire and Oxfordshire Marriage Bonds 1617-38' (*Journal of Berkshire, Buckinghamshire and Oxfordshire Arch. Soc.* vol. 2, 1896)

Place Names

MAWER, A., and STENTON, F. M., *The English Place Name Society vol. 2: Buckinghamshire* (1925)

Quarter Sessions

HARDY, W. C., and RECKITT, G. L., (eds.), *Calendar of Quarter Sessions Records* vols. 1-5 covers the period 1678-1724 (1933-58)

School Registers

HARWOOD, T., *Alumni Etonienses, or, a Catalogue of the Provosts and Fellows of Eton College* (1797)
STERRY, W., *The Eton College Register 1441-1698* (1943)

Visitations

METCALFE, W. C., (ed.), *The Heralds' Visitation of Buckinghamshire, 1566* (1883)
RYLANDS, W. H., (ed.), 'The Visitation of 1566' (*Harleian Society*, vol. 58, 1909)

General

Tracing your Buckinghamshire Ancestors (Buckinghamshire Family History Society, 1977)

Cambridgeshire

Record Repositories and Libraries

Cambridge County Record Office, Shire Hall, Castle Hill, Cambridge
Cambridge University Library, West Road, Cambridge (houses Ely diocesan
   records)
FARRAR, MICHAEL, *Genealogical Sources in Cambridgeshire* (1979)

Episcopal Registers and Registers of Clergy

Ely: Registers extant from 1337, except 1361-74, 1425-55, 1478-86, 1500-15.
CROSBY, J. H., 'Abstracts of the Registers from 1337-92' (*Ely Diocesan
   Remembrancer*, Nov. 1889-June 1900)
GIBBONS, A., *Ely Episcopal Records: A Calendar and Concise View of the Episcopal
   Records* (1891)
OWEN, D. M., *A Catalogue of the Records of the Bishop and Archdeacon of Ely* (1971)

Feet of Fines

RYE, W., (ed.), 'Feet of Fines for Cambridgeshire, 1195-1485' (*Cambridge
   Antiquarian Society Journal*, vol. 26, 1891)
see also Bedfordshire entry above

Heraldry

SUMMERS, PETER, (ed.), *Hatchments in Britain, vol. 6: Cambs., Essex, Herts.,
   Hunts. and Middlesex* (1985)

Marriage Licences

For 1562-82 *see* Gibbons, above
'Cambridgeshire Marriage Licences, 1582-99' (*Northern Genealogist*, vol. 1)

Parochial and Non-Parochial Registers

PALGRAVE-MOORE, P. (ed.), *National Index of Parish Registers vol. 7, Norfolk,
   Suffolk and Cambs.* (1983)

Pedigrees

ARMYTAGE, G. J., (ed.), *The Genealogist*, n. s. vol. 15, 1898
METCALFE, W. C., (ed.), 'Pedigrees of Cambridge families from the
   Visitation of 1683' (*The Genealogist*, vol. 3, 1879)

Place Names

REANEY, P. H., (ed.), *The English Place Name Survey, vol. 19: Cambridgeshire and Ely* (1943)

Subsidies

PALMER, W. M., (ed.), *Cambridgeshire Subsidy Rolls, 1250-1695* (1912: reprinted from the *East Anglian*, 1898-1909)

PALMER, W. M., (ed.), *Cambridge Borough Documents* (Cambridge Borough Council 1931). Vol. 1 contains Cambridge Poll Tax

Monumental Inscriptions

LAYER, J., and PALMER, W. M., (eds.), 'Monumental Inscriptions and Coats of Arms from Cambridgeshire' (*Cambridge Antiquarian Society*, vol. 34, 1932)

Visitations

CLAY, J. W., (ed.), 'The Visitations of 1575 and 1619' (*Harleian Society*, vol. 41, 1897)

Wills and Administrations

GRAY, G. J., *Abstracts of Wills ... of printers, binders and stationers of Cambridge, 1504-1699*

Calendar of Wills proved at the Vice-Chancellor's Court of the University of Cambridge, 1501-1765 (1907)

OWEN, D. M., *A Catalogue of the Records of the Bishop and Archdeacon of Ely* (1971)

Cheshire

Record Repositories and Libraries

Cheshire Record Office, The Castle, Chester
Chester City Record Office, Town Hall, Chester

Episcopal Registers and Records of Clergy

Chester Registers are extant from 1541.

GASTRELL, F., *Notitia Cestrensis, or, historical notices of the Diocese of Chester*, ed. F. R. Haines (*Camden Society*, o.s. vols. 8, 19, 21, 22, 1845-50)

IRVINE, W. F. A., (ed.), 'List of the clergy ... 1541-2' (*Lancashire and Cheshire Record Society*, vol. 33, 1896)
IRVINE, W. F. A., (ed.), 'The earliest Ordination Book of the Diocese of Chester, 1542-7 and 1555-8' (*L.C.R.S.*, vol. 43, 1902)

Feet of Fines

'Calendar of the Feet of Fines of Edward I for Cheshire' (*London Reports of the Deputy Keeper of the Public Record Office*, 1867)

Freemen

BENNETT, J. H. E., (ed.), 'Rolls of the Freemen of the City of Chester' (*L.C. R. S.*, vols. 51 and 55, 1906, 1908)

Inquisitiones Post Mortem

'Index nominum inquisitiones post mortem, Edward I–Charles I' (*R. D. K., P. R.O.*, 1864)
STEWARD-BROWN, R., (ed.), 'Cheshire Inquisitiones Post Mortem ... 1603-60' (*L.C. R. S.*, vols. 84, 86, 91, 1934-8)

Marriage Licences

Guide to Merrell's Marriage Index of Cheshire, 1580-1837 (1970)
IRVINE, W. F. A., (ed.), 'Marriage Licences granted within the archdeaconry of Chester and within the diocese of Chester, 1606-1700' (*L. C. R. S.*, vols. 53, 56, 57, 61, 65, 69, 73, 77, 1907-24)

Pedigrees

ADAMS, A., 'Cheshire Visitation Pedigrees, 1663' (*Harleian Society*, vol. 93, 1941)

Place Names

DODGSON, J. McN., (ed.), *The English Place Names Survey*, vols. 44, 45, 46, 47, 48, 54, 55: Cheshire (1970-present)

Quarter Sessions

BENNETT, J. H. E., and DEWHURST, J. C., (eds.), 'Quarter Sessions Records ... 1559-1760' (*L. C. R. S.*, vol. 94, 1940)

Visitations

ARMYTAGE, G. J., and RYLANDS, J. P., (eds.), 'The Visitation of 1613' (*Harleian Society*, vol. 59, 1909) Also issued as *L. C. R. S.*, vol. 58, 1909
RYLANDS, J. P., (ed.), 'The Visitations of 1533, 1566 and 1580' (*Harleian Society*, vol. 18, 1882)

Wills and Administrations

DICKINSON, R., (ed.), 'Wills proved at Chester, 1826-1830' (Phillimore & Co. Ltd. for the Record Society of Lancashire and Cheshire, *Record Series*, vol. 113, 1972)
DICKINSON, F., and R., (eds.), *Index to Wills and Administrations formerly preserved in the Probate Registry, Chester* (1978)
EARWAKER, J. P., (ed.), 'Lancashire and Cheshire Wills and Inventories at Chester, with an appendix of abstracts from wills now lost or destroyed' (*Camden Society*, o. s. vols. 3, 28, 37, 1884-97)
IRVINE, W. F. A., (ed.), 'An Index of Wills proved at Chester, 1487-1620' (*L. C. R. S.*, vol. 33, 1896)
PICCOPE, G. J., (ed.), 'Lancashire and Cheshire Wills and Inventories from the Ecclesiastical Courts of Chester' (*Camden Society*, o. s. vols. 33, 51, 54, 1887-61)
PRICE, W. H., (ed.), 'An Index of Wills proved at Chester, 1621-1700' (*L. C. R. S.*, vol. 43, 1902)
PRICE, W. H. (ed.), 'An Index of Wills proved at Chester, 1700-1800' (*L. C. R. S.*, vol. 52, 1905)
'An Index to the Wills and Inventories now preserved in the Court of Probate at Chester, 1545-1820' (*L. C. R. S.*, vols. 2, 4, 15, 18, 20, 22, 25, 37, 38, 44, 45, 62, 63, 78, 79, 1879-1928)

Cornwall

Record Repositories and Libraries

Cornwall County Record Office, County Hall, Truro
Royal Institution of Cornwall, River Street, Truro

Family Histories

PEDLER, SIR FREDERICK, *A Pedler Family History* (1984)
RIDOUT, ADELAIDE, *The Treffry Family* (1984)

Feet of Fines

see entry for Bedfordshire above

Genealogy

ROGERS, P., *Cornish Genealogy* (1954)

Hearth Tax Rolls

'The Hearth Tax Rolls for 1662' (*Devon and Cornwall Record Society Publications*, vol. 4, 1910)

Heraldry

BARING-GOULD, S., and TWIGGE, R., *An armoury of the Western Counties, Devon and Cornwall, from Exeter MSS of the 16th century* (1898)
JEWERS, A. J., *Heraldic church notes from Cornwall* (1889)
PASCOE, W. H., *A Cornish Armory*
WILLIAMS, B. H., *Ancient West Country (Devon and Cornwall) families and their armorial bearings* (1916)

Inquisitiones Post Mortem

FRY, H. A., (ed.), 'Cornish Inquisitiones Post Mortem, 1216-1649' (*D.C.R.S.*, vol. 1, 1906)

Muster Rolls

'Muster Rolls, 1569', *Devon and Cornwall Record Society Publications*, vol. 4, 1910

Parochial and Non-Parochial Registers

EDWARDS, L.W.L., *Index to Cornish Nonconformist Registers* (1976)
NICHOLLS, J., 'Index to parish register transcripts at Exeter and Bodmin' (*Journal of the Royal Institution of Cornwall*, vol. 19)

Subsidies

'Subsidies 1326-1660', *Devon and Cornwall Record Society Publications*, vol. 4, 1910

Visitations

VIVIAN, J.L., *The Visitations of Cornwall, 1530, 1573, 1620* (1887)
VIVIAN, J.L., and DRAKE, H.H., (eds.), 'The Visitation of 1620' (*Harleian Society*, vol. 9, 1874)

Wills and Administrations

CROSS, R.M., (ed.), 'Calendar of Wills and Administrations in the Archi-
diaconal Court of Cornwall, 1569-1699' (*British Record Society*, vol. 56, 1929)
CROSS, R.M., (ed.), 'Calendar of Wills and Administrations in the Archi-
diaconal Court of Cornwall, 1700-1799' (*British Record Society*, vol. 59, 1932)
'Probate Calendar of St Constantine 1570-1808' *Devon and Cornwall Record Society
Publications*, vol. 4, 1910
TRUDGIA, T.P.F., *Cornish Wills and Administrations at Somerset House and Exeter,
copied from the Glencross Card Index*

Cumberland

Record Repositories and Libraries

Cumbria Record Office, The Castle, Carlisle
Cumbria Record Office, County Offices, Kendal LA9 4RQ
Cumbria Record Office, 140 Duke Street, Barrow-in-Furness LA14 1XW
Cathedral Library, The Fratry, Carlisle Cathedral
HODGSON, H.W., *Bibliography of the History and Topography of Cumberland and
Westmorland* (Joint Archives Committee for Cumberland, Westmorland and
Carlisle, 1968)
Guide to Family History Records and Sources in Cumbria (Cumbria Record Office,
forthcoming)

Episcopal Registers and Registers of Clergy

Carlisle Registers are extant from 1292 except for 1396-1541.
'Register of John de Halton, 1292-1324' *Cumberland and Westmorland Antiquarian
and Archaeological Society* vol. 13, 1913.

Feet of Fines

see entry for Bedfordshire above

Heraldry

'Index to the Heraldry of Cumberland and Westmorland' (*C.W.A.A.S.*, vol. 6,
1905)
SUMMERS, PETER, (ed.), *Hatchments in Britain: vol. 3, The Northern Counties*
(1979)

Parochial and Non-Parochial Registers

WHITEHEAD, H., 'Cumberland Parish Registers' (*C.W.A.A.S.*, vol. 14, 1914)

Pedigrees

FOSTER, J., *Cumberland Pedigrees recorded in 1615 and...1616* (1924)

Place Names

ARMSTRONG, A.M., MAWER, A., STENTON, F.M., and DICKENS, B., (eds.), *The English Place-Name Society*, vols. 20, 21, 22: *Cumberland* (1950, 1950, 1952)

School Registers

ROUTLEDGE, G.B., (ed.), *Carlisle Grammar School Memorial Register, 1264-1924* (1924)

Subsidies

STEEL, J.P., *The Cumberland Lay Subsidy, 1332* (1910)

Visitations

LONGSTAFFE, W.H.D., (ed.), *The Visitation of 1530* (1863)
FETHERSTON, J., (ed.), 'The Visitation of 1615' (*Harleian Society*, vol. 7, 1872)

Wills and Administrations

FERGUSON, R. S., (ed.), *Testamenta Karleoniensia; the series of wills from the pre-reformation registers of the Bishop of Carlisle, 1355-86* (*C.W.A.A.S.*, extra series vol. 9, 1893)

Channel Islands

Record Repositories and Libraries

The Registrar General, The States Office, Royal Square, Jersey (Civil Registration since 1942, closed to researchers)

Société Jersiaise, The Library, The Museum, 9 Pier Road, Jersey (by appointment with the Librarian)
The Registrar-General, The Greffe, St Peter Port, Guernsey (Postal enquiries only) (also holds records for Alderney and Sark)

MARR, L. J., *Guernsey People* (1984)
Transactions of La Société Guernesiaise
DE SAUSMAREZ, C., *The Story of William le Marchant* (1965)
SMITH-KELLETT, S., *Restaud of Jethou* (1969)
SARRE, A. C., *Sarre* 1957)
CURTIS, C., *The Seals of the Royal Court of Guernsey* (1939)
LANGTON, C., 'Records and Record Searching in Jersey' (*Genealogists Magazine* V, p. 314, 1931)
PAYNE, J. B., *An Armorial of Jersey: an account, heraldic and antiquarian, of the chief native families with pedigrees, biographical notes etc.* (several volumes, unfinished, 1859-65)

Derbyshire

Record Repositories and Libraries

Derbyshire Record Office, County Offices, Matlock DE4 3AG
Chesterfield Public Library, Corporation St., Chesterfield
Derby Central Library, Wardwick, Derby
RIDEN, P., *How to trace your ancestors in Derbyshire* (1982)

Feet of Fines

see Bedfordshire entry above

Hearth Tax Assessments

EDMONDS, D.G., (ed.), *Derbyshire Hearth Tax Assessments 1662-70* (1982)

Parochial and Non-Parochial Registers

MARSHALL, G. W., (ed.)'Derbyshire Funeral Certificates, 1631-97' (*The Genealogist*, vol. 7, 1883)
MARSHALL, G. W., (ed.), 'Derbyshire Funeral Certificates, 1619-45' (*The Genealogist*, n.s. vols. 1-2, 1884-5)
MARSHALL, G. W., (ed.), 'Lists of Derbyshire Funeral Certificates' (*The Genealogist*, n.s. vols. 12-13, 1895-6)

Place Names

CAMERON, K., (ed.), *The English Place Name Survey, vols. 27, 28, 29: Derbyshire* (1959)

Roman Catholic Records

CLARK, RICHARD, (ed.), *The Derbyshire Papist Returns of 1705-6* (1982)

School Registers

TACHELLA, B., (ed.), *The Derby School Register, 1570-1901* (1902)
MESSITER, M., (ed.), *Repton School Register, 1557-1910* (1910)

Subsidies

'The subsidy of 1327-8' (*Derbyshire Archaeological and Natural History Society*, vol. 30, c.1908)

Devon

Record Repositories and Libraries

Devon Record Office, Castle Street, Exeter EX4 3PQ
Exeter Cathedral Library, The Bishop's Palace, Exeter
West Devon Area Record Office, Clare Place, Coxside, Plymouth

Directories

WHITE, W., *Gazetteer and Directory of Devonshire and the City and County of Exeter* (modern reprint of 1850 original)

Episcopal Records and Records of Clergy

Exeter registers are extant from 1257, except 1291-1307 and 1646-60.
HINGESTON-RANDOLPH, F.C., (ed.) *Episcopal Registers of the Diocese of Exeter* (1886-1915), covers the following registers: Walter Bronescombe (1257-80); Peter Quivil (1280-91); Thomas de Bytton (1292-1307); Walter de Stapledon (1307-26); James de Berkeley (1327); Thomas de Brantyngham (1370-94); Edmund Stafford (1395-1419); Edmund Lacy (1420-55).
HORN, J.M., (ed.), *Fasti Ecclesiae Anglicanae: Diocese of Exeter 1300-1541* (1965)

Feet of Fines

see Bedfordshire entry above
REICHEL, O.J., (ed.), 'Feet of Fines for Devonshire, 1196-1369' (*Devon and Cornwall Record Society*, vol. 6, (2 vols.), 1912-1939)

Heraldry

see Cornwall entry above

Inquisitiones Post Mortem

FRY, H.A., (ed.) 'Calendar of Devonshire Inquisitiones Post Mortem' (*D.C.R.S.* vol. 1, 1906)

Manorial Records

'A complete list of manorial documents in Exeter City Library' (*Bulletin of the Institute of Historical Research*, vols. 9 and 10, 1932-3, 1933-4)

Marriage Licences

VIVIAN, J.L., (ed.), *The Bishop's Registry at Exeter, 1523-1632* (1887-9)
VIVIAN, J.L., (ed.), 'Additions to the Bishop's Registry at Exeter, 1598-9' (*Devon and Cornwall Notes and Queries*, 1919)
Devon and Cornwall. Marriage Licences of Diocese of Exeter. 1631-68. (Typescript at Society of Genealogists)
MANN, J.H., (ed.), 'Devon and Cornwall Marriage Allegations Index, 1660-1733' (*Society of Genealogists*, typescript at Society of Genealogists)

Militia and Muster Rolls

HOSKINS, W.G., *The Exeter Militia List, 1803* (1972)
HOWARD, A.J. and STOATE, T.C., *The Devon Muster Rolls for 1569* (1977)

Monumental Inscriptions

'Monumental Inscriptions at Bickleigh' (*The Genealogist*, vol. 5, 1881)
'Monumental Inscriptions at Idysleigh and Dowland' (*The Genealogist*, vol. 7, 1883)

Parochial and Non-Parochial Registers

DICKINSON, F.B., 'Our Parish Registers', (*Exeter Diocesan &c Society*, 3rd series, vol. 2)

GRANVILLE, R.R., and MUGFORD, W.E., *Abstracts of the existing transcripts of the lost parish registers of Devonshire, 1596-1644*, vol. 1, A-Bra (1908)

PHILLIMORE, W.P.W., (ed.), *Devonshire Parish Registers* (1909)

'Transcripts of parish registers, bishops' transcripts, etc., in the possession of the Society', (*D.C.R.S.*, vol. 22, 1948)

Place Names

GOVER, J.E.B., MAWER, A., and STENTON, F.M., (eds.), *The English Place Name Society, vols. 8 and 9: Devon* (1931)

Quarter Sessions

HAMILTON, A.H.A., *Devon Quarter Sessions from Queen Elizabeth to Queen Anne* (1878)

Visitations

COLBY, F.T., (ed.), *Visitation of the County of Devon, 1564* (1881)

COLBY, F. T., (ed.), *Visitation of the County of Devon, 1620* (Harleian Society Publication, vol. 6, 1872)

VIVIAN, J.H., (ed.), *Visitations of the County of Devon, 1531, 1564 and 1620* (1895)

Wills and Administrations

FRY, E.A., (ed.), 'Calendar of Devon and Cornwall Wills, 1540-1799' (*Index Library*, vol. 35, 1908)

FRY, E.A., (ed.), 'Calendar of Devon Wills, Consistory Court Exeter, 1532-1800' (*Index Library*, vol. 46, 1914)

WORTHY, L., *Devonshire Wills: A Collection of Annotated Testamentary Abstracts, 1413-1878* (1896)

'Notes on the Exeter District Probate Registry' (*Devon Association*, 1901)

Dorset

Record Repositories and Libraries

Dorset Record Office, County Hall, Dorchester DT1 1XJ

Feet of Fines

see Bedfordshire entry above
FRY, E.A., and FRY, G.S., (eds.), 'Abstracts of Dorset Feet of Fines, 1195-1485'
(*Dorset Records*, vols. 5, 10, 1898, 1903)

Inquisitiones Post Mortem

FRY, E.A., 'On the Inquisitiones Post Mortem for Dorset, 1216-1484'
(*Proceedings of the Dorset Natural History and Antiquarian Society*, vol. 17, 1896)
FRY, E.A., 'On the Inquisitiones Post Mortem for Dorset, 1485-1648'
(*P.D.N.H.A.S.*, vol. 20, 1899)
FRY, E.A., 'On the Inquisitiones Post Mortem for Dorset' (*Somerset and Dorset Notes and Queries*, vol. 8, 1908)

Pedigrees

ARMYTAGE, G.J., *Pedigrees from the Visitation of Dorsetshire, 1531* (1906)

Place Names

MILLS, A.D., (ed.), *The English Place Name Society, vols. 52, 53: Dorset* (1977, 1981)

Tax Assessments

MEEKINGS, C.A.F., *Dorset Hearth Tax Assessments, 1662-4* (1961)

Visitations

BYSSHE, SIR EDWARD, (ed.), 'The Visitation of Dorset, 1677' (*Harleian Society*, vol. 17, 1882)
METCALFE, W.C., (ed.), 'The Visitation of Dorset, 1565' (*The Genealogist*, n.s., vols. 2-3, 1885-6)
RYLANDS, J.P., (ed.), 'The Visitation of Dorset, 1623' (*Harleian Society*, vol. 20, 1885)

Wills and Administrations

FRY, E.A., (ed.), 'A Calendar of Wills and Administrations, 1568-1799' (*British Record Society, Index Library*, vol. 22, 1900)
FRY, G.S., (ed.), 'A Calendar of Wills and Administrations relating to the County of Dorset' (*British Record Society, Index Library*, vol. 53, 1922)

'Calendar of Dorset Wills proved in the Prerogative Court of Canterbury, 1383-1700' (*Dorset Records*, vol. 2, 1894)
EVERETT, C.R., 'Testamentary Papers at Sarum' (*The Genealogist's Magazine*, vol. 5, 1929-31)

Durham

Record Repositories and Libraries

Durham County Record Office, County Hall, Durham DH1 5UL
University of Durham, Department of Paleography and Diplomatic, The Prior's Kitchen, The College, Durham DH1 3EQ; and 5 The College, Durham DH1 3EQ
Durham Cathedral Library, The College, Durham
University Library, Palace Green, Durham
Gateshead Central Library, Prince Consort Road, Gateshead NE8 4LN

Episcopal Registers and Records of Clergy

Durham registers are extant from 1311 except for 1317-33
BOUTFLOWER, D.S., (ed.), 'Fasti Dunelmenses: A Record of the Beneficed Clergy of the Diocese to the Dissolution of the Monastic and Collegiate Churches' (*Surtees Society*, vol. 139, 1926)
GREENWELL, W., (ed.), 'Bishop Hatfield's Survey, 1345-81' (*Surtees Society*, vol. 32, 1857)
HARDY, T.D., (ed.), *Registrum Palatinum Dunelmense. Register of Richard de Kellawe, 1314-16* (Rolls Series, 4 vols., 1873-8)
HOWDEN, M.P., (ed.), 'Register of Richard Fox, 1494-1501' (*Surtees Society*, vol. 147, 1932)
'Indexes to Persons and Places in Kellawe's Register' (R.D.K.P.R.O., vol. 30, pp. 99-120, 1869)
KITCHEN, G.W., (ed.), 'Richard d'Aungerville and Bury: Fragments of his Register, 1338-45' (*Surtees Society*, vol. 119, 1910)
'Presentations to Benefices during the Interregnum' (*Proceedings of the Society of Antiquaries of Newcastle*, 4th series, vol. 46, 1916)
STOREY, R.L., (ed.), 'Register of Thomas Langley, 1406-37' (*Surtees Society*, vol. 164, 1956)

Feet of Fines

OLIVER, A.M., and JOHNSON, C., (eds.), *Feet of Fines for Northumberland and Durham, 1196-1272* (Newcastle-upon-Tyne Records Committee, publication no. 10, 1933)

Heraldry

SUMMERS, PETER, (ed.), *Hatchments in Britain: vol. 3, The Northern Counties* (1980)

Inquisitiones Post Mortem

'Calendar of Inquisitiones Post Mortem, 1318-1639' (44 and 45 R.D.K., P.R.O. 1882 and 1883)

Parochial and Non-Parochial Registers

NEAT, C.P. (ed.), *National Index of Parish Registers, vol. XI pt. 1: Northumberland and Durham* (1980)

WOOD, H.M., 'List of Parochial and Non-Parochial Registers Relating to Durham and Northumberland' (*Durham and Northumberland Parish Register Society*, vol. 26, 1898)

Visitations

FOSTER, J., (ed.), *Pedigrees recorded at the visitations...of Durham...1575...1615...1666* (1887)

Wills and Administrations

WOOD, H.M., *Index of Wills, etc., in the Probate Registry, Durham, and from other sources, 1540-99* (Newcastle-upon-Tyne Records Committee, publication no. 8, 1928)

Essex

Record Repositories and Libraries

Colchester Public Library, Sherwell Road, Colchester

Colchester and Essex Museum, The Castle, Colchester, houses the library of the Essex Archaeological Society

Essex Record Office, Block A, County Hall, King Edward Avenue, Chelmsford CM1 1LX

Essex Record Office (Southend Branch), Central Library, Victoria Avenue, Southend-on-Sea

EMMISON, F.G., *Catalogue of Essex Parish Records, 1240-1894* EMMISON, F.G., *Guide to the Essex Record Office* (2nd edn., 1969)

Many Essex Record Office publications

Feet of Fines

Vol I, 1182-1272; vol II, 1272-1355-65, vol. III, 1327-1422, vol. IV, 1423-1547
(*Essex Archaeological Society*, 1899-1964)

Heraldry

see Cambridgeshire entry

Pedigrees

BERRY, W., *County Pedigrees: Pedigrees of Essex Families* (1840)

Place Names

REANEY, P.H., (ed.), *The English Place Name Society, vol. 12: Essex* (1935)

Quarter Sessions

ALLEN, D.H., (ed.), *Essex Quarter Sessions Order Book, 1652-1661* (1974)

Visitations

HOWARD, J.J., (ed.), *The Visitation of the County of Essex, 1664-8* (1888)
METCALFE, W.C., (ed.), 'Visitations of Essex, 1552 and 1558' (*Harleian Society*, vol. 13, 1878)
METCALFE, W.C., (ed.) 'Visitations of Essex, 1570 and 1612' (*Harleian Society*, vol. 14, 1879)

Wills and Administrations

EMMISON, F.G., (ed.), 'Wills at Chelmsford, 1400-1619' (*British Record Society*, vol. 78, 1957)
EMMISON, F.G., (ed.), 'Wills at Chelmsford, 1620-1720' (*B.R.S.*, vol. 79, 1958)
EMMISON, F.G., (ed.), 'Wills at Chelmsford, 1721-1858' (*B.R.S.*, vol. 84, 1969)
'Abstracts of early Essex Wills, 1377-1658' (*Transactions of the Essex Archaeological Society*, vols. 1-4; n.s. vols. 1-3)

General Interest

ADDISON, SIR W., *Essex Worthies* (1973)
BROWN, A., *Essex People, 1750-1900* (1972)

EMMISON, F.G., *Elizabethan Life*: vol. I, *Disorder* (1970); vol. II, *Morals and the Church Courts* (1973); vol. III, *Home and Work* (1976); vol. IV, *Essex Gentry's Wills in the P.C.C.* (1978); vol. V, *Wills of Essex Gentry and Yeomen* (1980)
STEER, F.W., (ed.), *Farm and Cottage Inventories of Mid-Essex* (1969)

Gloucestershire (including Bristol)

Record Repositories and Libraries

Bristol Archives Office, The Council House, College Green, Bristol
Gloucestershire Record Office, Kingsholm, Worcester Street, Gloucester GL1 3DW
Gloucester City Library, Brunswick Road, Gloucester (contains large local history collection, the 'Gloucestershire Collection')
Gloucester Cathedral Library, The Cathedral, Gloucester
Tracing your Ancestors in Gloucestershire (Gloucestershire Record Office)
Gloucestershire Family History (1979)

Censuses

RALPH, ELIZABETH, and WILLIAMS, MARY E., *The Inhabitants of Bristol in 1696*

Emigrants

HARGREAVES-MAUDSLEY, R., *Bristol and America: A Record of the First Settlers in the Colonies of America, 1654-85* (1978 reprint of 1931 edn.)

Episcopal Registers and Records of Clergy

Bristol registers are extant from 1541
BOSWELL, E., *The Ecclesiastical Division of the Diocese of Bristol, with Lists of Dignitaries* (c.1825)
Gloucester registers are extant from 1541: for episcopal records before that date, see under Worcestershire below.

Feet of Fines

AUSTIN, R., (ed.), *Catalogue of the Gloucestershire Collection in Gloucester Public Library* (Gloucester Public Library, 1928)

MACLEAN, J., 'Pedes Finium, 1205-72' (*Transactions of the Bristol and Gloucester-shire Archaeological Society*, vol. 16, 1891-2)
MACLEAN, J., 'Pedes Finium, 1587-1623' (*T.B.G.A.S.*, vol. 17, 1892-3)

Heraldry

AUSTIN, R., 'Coats of Arms of Gloucestershire' *Notes and Queries*, series 12, vol. 7, 1920)
NAYLOR, SIR G., *A Collection of the Coats of Arms borne by the Nobility and Gentry of the County of Gloucester* (1792)
WERE, F., 'Index to the Heraldry in Bigland's *List of Gloucestershire*' (*T.B.G.A.S.*, vol. 28, 1905)

Inquisitiones Post Mortem

MADGE, S.J., (ed.), 'Abstracts of Gloucestershire Inquisitiones Post Mortem, 1236-1413' (*British Record Society Index Library*, vols. 30, 40, 47, 1903-14)
PHILLIMORE, W.P.W., (ed.), 'Abstracts of Gloucestershire Inquisitiones Post Mortem, 1625-42' (*B.R.S.I.L.*, vols. 9, 13, 21, 1893-9)
'Gloucestershire Inquisitiones Post Mortem vol. I, Charles I 1-11' (*B.R.S.I.L.*, vol. 9, 1893)
    vol. II, Charles I 12-20 (*B.R.S.I.L.*, vol. 13, 1895)
    vol. III, miscellaneous Charles I (*B.R.S.I.L.*, vol. 21, 1899)
    vol. IV, 1236-1300 (*B.R.S.I.L.*, vol. 30, 1903)
    vol. V, 1302-58 (*B.R.S.I.L.*, vol. 40, 1910)
    vol. VI, 1359-1413 (*B.R.S.I.L.*, vol. 47, 1914)

Marriage Allegations

FRITH, B., *Gloucestershire Marriage Allegations, 1637-80* (with Surrogate Allega-tions to 1694) (1954)
FRITH, B., *Gloucestershire Marriage Allegations, 1681-1700* (1971)
RALPH, E., (ed.), *Marriage Bonds for the Diocese of Bristol, vol. I, 1637-1700* (1954)
Bristol Marriages 1800-37: part 1 (Bristol and Avon Family History Society)

Members of Parliament

WILLIAMS, W.R., *Parliamentary History of the County of Gloucester, 1213-1898* (1898)

Musters

SMITH, J., *Names and Surnames of all...men fit to serve in the Wars, within the County of Gloucester, 1608* (1902)

Monumental Inscriptions

'Monumental Inscriptions at Prestbury' (*The Genealogist*, vol. 2, 1878)
'Monumental Inscriptions at Longney; St Peter's, Cheltenham; Cubberley; Great Witcombe' (*The Genealogist*, vol. 3, 1879)

Parochial and Non-Parochial Registers

GRAY, I.E., and RALPH, E., (eds.), *Guide to the parish records of the City of Bristol and the County of Gloucester* (Bristol and Gloucestershire Archaeological Society Records Section, no. 5, 1963)

GRAY, I., and GETHYN-JONES, E., (eds.), *The Registers of the Church of St Mary Dymock, 1538-1790* (1960)

STEEL, D. J., et al (eds.), *National Index of Parish Registers* vol. V: The South Midlands and the Welsh Borders (1966, reprinted 1976)

Place Names

SMITH, A.H., (ed.), *The English Place Name Society, vols. 38, 39, 40, 41: Gloucestershire* (1964-5)

Quarter Sessions

GRAY, I.E., and GAYDON, A.T., *Gloucestershire Quarter Sessions Archives, 1660-1889, and other official records* (Gloucestershire County Council, 1958)

Subsidy Rolls

PHILLIPS, T., (ed.), *Gloucestershire Subsidy Roll...1327* (privately printed, 1856)

Visitations

FENWICK, T.F., and METCALFE, W.C., *Visitation of the County of Gloucester, 1682-3* (1884)

MACLEAN, J., and HEARNE, W.C., *Visitations of Gloucestershire, 1569, 1582-3, 1623* (*Harleian Society*, vol. 21, 1885)

Wills and Administrations

DICKINSON, M.G., *Wills Proved in the Gloucestershire Peculiar Courts* (Local History Pamphlet No. 2)

FRY, E.A., (ed.), 'Calendar of Wills proved in the Consistory Court of Bristol, 1572-1792';'Calendar of Wills proved in the Great Orphan Books, 1379-1674' (*British Record Society Index Library*, vol. 17, 1897)

PHILLIMORE, W.P.W., (ed.), 'Calendar of Gloucestershire Wills': vol. I, 1541-1650 (*British Record Society Index Library*, vol. 12, 1895); vol. II, 1660-1880 (*British Record Society Index Library*, vol. 34, 1907)

MOORE, J., *The Goods and Chattels of our Forefathers: Probate Inventories for Frampton Cotterell and District* (1976)

Hampshire and the Isle of Wight

EDWARDS, F.H., and E., *Guide to Genealogical Sources in Hampshire* (1983)

Record Repositories and Libraries

Hampshire Record Office, 20 Southgate Street, Winchester SO23 9EF
Isle of Wight County Record Office, 26 Hillside, Newport
Portsmouth City Record Office, 3 Museum Road, Portsmouth PO1 2LE
Southampton Civic Record Office, Civic Centre, Southampton SO9 4XL
Winchester City Record Office, Guildhall, Winchester
Winchester Cathedral Library, The Cathedral, Winchester

Apprenticeship Records

WILLIS, ARTHUR J., *A Calendar of Southampton Apprenticeship Registers 1609-1740* (1968)

Censuses

The *Hampshire Genealogical Society* has published a series of Indexes to the 1851 Census.

Vol. 1: Nursling, Timsbury, Michelmersh, Mottisfont, East Wellow, Sherfield English, Lockerley, East Dean

Vol. 2: Newnham, Nately Scures, Up Nately, Upton Grey, Weston Patrick, Weston Corbett, Tunworth, Basingstoke

Vol. 3: Hunton, Wonston, Avington, Sparsholt, Micheldever, Headbourne Worthy, Stoke Charity, East Stratton, Martyr Worthy, Laston, Crawley, Littleton, Kingsworthy, Itchen Abbas

Vol. 4: Amport, Goodworth Clatford, Wherwell, Longparish, Chilbolton, Upper Clatford, Barton Stacey, Bullington, Abbotts Ann

Vol. 5: Worting, Monk Sherbourne, Pamber, Wootton St Lawrence, Bramley, Silchester, Church Oakley, Deane

Vol. 6: Sherfield-on-Loddon, Sherborne St John, Stratfield Turgis, Basing, Andwell, Eastrop, Winslade, Stratfield Saye, Hartley Wespall, Mapledurwell

Vol. 7: Preston Candover, Farleigh Wallop, North Waltham, Woodmancott, Cliddesden, Ellisfield, Steventon, Herriard, Bradley, Dummer, Nutley, Popham

Vol. 8: Andover, Penton Mewsey, Foxcott, Monxton, Penton Grafton

Vol. 9: Kingsclere, Ewhurst, Hannington, Wolverton, Sydmonton, Baughurst, Ecchinswell

Vol. 10: East Woodhay, Ashmansworth, Crux Easton, Woodcott, Litchfield, Burghclere, Tadley, Highclere

Vol. 11: Chilcomb, Morestead, Owlesbury, Twyford, Compton

Vol. 12: Bishopstoke, Hursley, Otterbourne, Farley Chamberlayne, North Baddesley

Vol. 13: Romsey

Vol. 14: St Mary Extra, Hound, Hamble-le-Rice, Bursledon, Botley, North Stoneham, Chilworth

Vol. 15: Beauworth, Bishop's Sutton, Bramdean, Cheriton, Hinton Ampner, Itchen Stoke, Kilmeston, Ovington, Ropley, Tichbourne, West Tisted

Vol. 16: South Storeham

Vol. 17: Overton, Ashe, Laverstoke, Freefolk, Whitchurch, Tufton, Hurstbourne Priors, St Mary Bourne

Vol. 18: Hayling South, Hayling North, Warblington, Havant, Bedhampton, Farlington

Directories

JAMES, J.F., (ed.), *Comyn's Directory of the New Forest, 1817* (facsimile edition incorporating the Boldre and Brockenhurst directories, 1982)

Episcopal Registers and Records of Clergy

Winchester registers are extant from 1282, except for 1616-1627 and 1642-1665

CHITTY, H., 'Registra Stephani Gardiner (et Johannis Poynet) 1531-51' (*Canterbury and York Society*, vol. 37, 1930)

DEEDES, C., 'Registrum Johannis de Pontissara, 1282-1304' (*C.Y.S.*, vols. 19 and 30, 1915, 1924)

FRERE, W.H., 'Registrum Johannis White, 1556-9' (*C.Y.S.*, vol. 16, 1914)

CHITTY, H., 'Registrum Thom. Wolsey, 1529-30' (*C.Y.S.*, vol. 32, 1926)

GOODMAN, A.W., 'Registrum Hen. Woodlock, 1306-16' (*C.Y.S.*, vols. 43 and 44, 1940 and 1941)

BAIBENT, C.J., 'Registers of John de Sandale and Reigand de Asserio...1316-23' (*Hampshire Record Society*, publication 8, 1897)

KIRBY, T.F., 'William of Wykeham's Register' (*Hampshire Record Society*, publication 11 (2 vols.) 1896, 1899)

BRIDGER, C., *Index to Printed Winchester Registers* (1867)

WILLIS, ARTHUR J., *Winchester Ordinations*: vol. 1, Ordinands' Papers 1734-1827 (1964); vol. 2, Bishop's Registers, Subscriptions Books and Exhibitions of Order (1965)

Marriage Licences

MOENS, W.J.C., 'Hampshire Allegations for Marriage Licences' 1689-1837, vol. I [Bridegrooms A-L] (1893), Vol. II [Bridegrooms M-Y] (1893) (*Harleian Society Publications*, vols. 35 and 36, supplemented by *Genealogist's Magazine*, vol. 14, nos. 2 and 3, pp. 48-55, 73-82, Society of Genealogists, June/Sept, 1962 (*Harleian Society*, vols. 35 and 36, 1893)

WILLIS, ARTHUR J., *Hampshire Marriage Licences 1607-40 from the records in the Diocesan Registry, Winchester* (1957)

WILLIS, ARTHUR J., *Hampshire Marriage Licences 1669-80 from the records in the Diocesan Registry, Winchester* (1963)

Isle of Wight, Index to marriages in 15 parishes

Miscellany

WILLIS, ARTHUR J., *A Hampshire Miscellany*: vol. 1, Metropolitical Visitation 1607-8 (1963); vol. 2, Laymen's Licences of the Diocese of Winchester 1675-1834 (1964); vol. 3, Dissenters' Meeting House Certificates, 1702-1844 (1964); vol. 4, Exhibit Books, Terriers and Episcopatus Redivivus (1967)

Parochial and Non-Parochial Registers

FEARSON, W.A., and WILLIAMS, J.E., *Parish registers and parochial documents in the Archdeaconry of Winchester, with an Appendix of Hampshire non-parochial registers* (1909)

'Hampshire Parish Registers' (*Hampshire Antiquary*, vol. 2)

Pedigrees

BERRY, W., *County Genealogies: Pedigrees of the Families in the County of Hampshire* (1833)

School Records

HIMSWORTH, SHEILA, (ed.), *Winchester College Muniments*: vol. 1 (1976); vol. 2 (1984); vol. 3 (1984)

Visitations

MARSHALL, G.W., *An Index to the Hampshire Pedigrees contained in the printed Heralds' Visitations* (1866)

RYLANDS, W.H., (ed.) 'Visitations of Hampshire, 1530, 1575 and 1622-4' (*Harleian Society*, vol. 64, 1913)

Wills and Administrations

WILLIS, ARTHUR J., (ed.) *Wills, Administrations and Inventories with the Winchester Diocesan Records* (1968)

Herefordshire

Record Repositories and Libraries

Cathedral Library and Muniment Room, The Cathedral, Hereford
Hereford and Worcester Record Office (Hereford branch), The Old Barracks, Harold Street, Hereford HR1 2QX
Hereford City Library, Broad Street, Hereford

Episcopal Registers and Records of Clergy

Hereford registers are extant from 1275, except 1492-1504 and 1586-1602
The *Canterbury and York Society*, in conjunction with the *Cantilupe Society*, has issued the following registers:
Thomas de Cantilupe, 1275-82 (vol. 2, 1907)
Richard de Swinfield, 1283-1317 (vol. 6, 1909)
Adam de Orleton, 1317-27 (vol. 5, 1908)
Thomas Charlton, 1327-44 (vol. 9, 1913)
John de Trillek, 1344-61 (vol. 8, 1912)
Lewis Charlton, 1361-70 (vol. 14, 1914)
William Courtenay, 1370-5 (vol. 18, 1914)
John Gilbert, 1375-9 (vol. 19, 1915)
John Trefnant, 1389-1404 (vol. 20, 1916)
Robert Mascall, 1404-17 (vol. 21, 1917)
Edmund Lacy, 1417-20 (vol. 22, 1918)
Thomas Poltone, 1420-2 (vol. 23, 1918)
Thomas Spofford, 1422-8 (vol. 24, 1919)
Richard Beauchamp, 1449-50 (vol. 25, 1920)
Richard Boulers, 1451-3 (vol. 26, 1920)
John Stanbury, 1453-74 (vol. 26, 1920)
Thomas Myllyng, 1474-92 (vol. 27, 1920)
Richard Mayew, 1504-16; Charles Bothe, 1516-35; Edward Fox, 1535-8 and Edmund Bonner, 1538-9 (vol. 28, 1921)
DEW, E.N., *Index to the Registers of the Diocese of Hereford, 1275-1535* (1925)

BANNISTER, A.T., 'Diocese of Hereford: Institutions, &c., 1539-1900'
(*Cantilupe Society*, vol. 2, 1923)
DEW, E.N. (ed.), *Extracts from the Cathedral Registers, 1275-1535* (1932)
HORN, J.M., (comp.), *Fasti Ecclesiae Anglicanae: Hereford Diocese 1300-1541* (1962)

Heraldry

STRONG, G., *The Heraldry of Herefordshire* (1848)

Members of Parliament

WILLIAMS, W.R., *The Parliamentary History of the County of Hereford, 1275-1896*
(1896)

Parochial and Non-Parochial Registers

see Gloucestershire entry

Visitations

WEAVER, F.W., (ed.), *The Visitation of Herefordshire...1569* (1886)

Wills and Administrations

'A list of wills in the Cause Books of the Bishops of Hereford, 1444-1578'
(*Miscellanea Genealogica et Heraldica*, 5th series vol. 4, 1920-2)

Hertfordshire

BOWDEN, R.A., *Genealogical Sources for Hertfordshire* (Hertfordshire Record
Office, 1972)

Record Repositories and Libraries

Hertfordshire County Record Office, County Hall, Hertford SG1 8DE
LE HARDY, WILLIAM, *A Guide to the Hertfordshire County Record Office: part 1,
Quarter Sessions and other Records in the Custody of the Officials* (1961)

Episcopal Registers and Records of Clergy

A typescript index of marriage licences at St Albans and Huntingdon
Archdeaconry

Family Histories

KING, NORAH, *The Grimstons of Gorhambury* (1983)

Feet of Fines

'Feet of Fines for Hertfordshire, 1485-1603' (*Hertfordshire Genealogist and Antiquary*,
vols. 1-3, 1895, 1896, 1897)
'Feet of Fines for Harpenden, 1509-1688' (*St Albans and Hertfordshire Architectural
and Archaeological Society*, 3rd series, vol. 38, 1932-4)

Heraldry

see Cambridgeshire entry

Inquisitiones Post Mortem

BRIGG, William (ed.),'List of Inquisitiones Post Mortem for Hertfordshire,
1485-1603' (*Hertfordshire Genealogist*, vol. 2, 1896)
BRIGG, William (ed.), 'Abstracts of some Inquisitiones Post Mortem for
Hertfordshire, Hen. VIII-Chas. I' (*Hertfordshire Genealogist*, vols. 3-4, 1897-8)

Manorial Records

'A list of manorial records in County Council Offices' (*Bulletin of the Institute of
Historical Research*, vol. 9, 1932)

Marriage Licences

BRIGG, William (ed.), 'Marriage Licences, Archdeaconry of St Albans,
1584-1715' (*H.G.*, vols. 1-3, 1895-7)
ALLEN, T.F., 'Marriage Licences, Archdeaconry of St Albans, 1715-1830, n.d.,
typescript in Herts. CRO
BRIGG, William (ed.), 'Marriage Licences, Archdeaconry of Hitchin, 1610-49'
(*H.G.*, vol. 2, 1896)
ALLEN, T.F., 'Marriage Licences, Archdeaconry of Hitchin, 1682-1685,
1756-1837, n.d. typescript in Herts. CRO

Muster Rolls

BRIGG, William (ed.), 'Provision of armour and men by the clergy of the
Archdeaconry of St Albans, 1590' (*H.G.*, vol. 1, 1895)
SAINSBURY, J.D., *Hertfordshire's Soldiers* (1969)

Parochial and Non-Parochial Registers

'The oldest Parish Registers of Hertfordshire' (*Middlesex and Hertfordshire Notes
and Queries*, vols. 3 and 4)
BRIGG, William (ed.), 'List of Transcripts of Registers for the Archdeaconry of
St Albans' (*H.G.*, vols. 1, 3, 1895, 1897)
BRIGG, William (ed.), 'List of Hertfordshire Non-Parochial Registers' (*H.G.*,
vol. 1, 1895)
BROWNING, D. J. (ed.), *Register of Rainford Chapel in the Parish of Prescot, marriages
1813-37* (1981)
RUSTON, A.R., *Bushey United Reformed Church: Registers and Monumental Inscriptions*
(1980)

Pedigrees

BERRY, W., *County Genealogies: Pedigrees of Hertfordshire Families* (1844)

Quarter Sessions

HARDY, W.J., and HARDY, W.L., (eds.), *Hertford County Records, 1581-1850* (9
vols., 1905-38)

Subsidies

BRIGG, William (ed.), 'Subsidy Rolls for Hertfordshire, 1545' (*H.G.*, vols. 1-2,
1895, 1896)
BRIGG, William (ed.), 'Subsidy Rolls for Hertfordshire, 1566-7' (*H.G.*, vol. 3,
1897)

Visitations

METCALFE, W.C., (ed.), 'Visitations of Hertfordshire, 1572, 1634' (*Harleian
Society*, vol. 22, 1886)

Wills and Administrations

'Abstracts of Wills from the Archdeaconry of St Albans, 1415-' (*H.G.*, vols. 1, 3,
1895, 1897)

'Abstracts of Wills from the Archdeaconry of Hitchin, 1579-1614' (*H.G.*, vols. 1,2,3, 1895-7)

BULLER, PHILIP and BARBARA, *Pots, Platters and Ploughs: Sarrat Wills and Inventories 1435-1832* (1984)

MUNBY, LIONEL, *Life and Death in King's Langley, 1498-1659* (probate inventories) (1981)

Huntingdonshire

Record Repositories and Libraries

Cambridge County Record Office (Huntingdon Branch), Grammar School Walk, Huntingdon   E18 6LF

FINDLAY, G.H., *Guide to the Huntingdonshire County Record Office* (Huntingdon County Council, 1958)

Feet of Fines

TURNER, G.J., 'Calendar of Feet of Fines for Huntingdonshire, 1194-1603' (*Cambridge Antiquarian Society*, No. 37, 8vo series, 1913)

Heraldry

see Cambridgeshire entry

Marriage Licences

NOBLE, W.M., (ed.) *Huntingdonshire Marriage Licences, 1517 and 1610-14*

This appendix of Huntingdonshire marriage licences is included in NOBLE, W.M., (ed.) 'Calendars of Huntingdonshire Wills, 1479-1652' (*British Record Society Index Library*, vol. 42, 1911)

Place Names

MAWER, A., and STENTON, F.M., (eds.), *The English Place Name Society, vol. 3: Bedfordshire and Huntingdonshire* (1926)

Visitations

ELLIS, H., (ed.) 'The Visitation of Huntingdonshire, 1613' (*Camden Society*, o.s. vol. 43, 1849)

Wills and Administrations

NOBLE, W.M., (ed.) 'Calendars of Huntingdonshire Wills, 1479-1652' (*British Record Society Index Library*, vol. 42, 1911)

Isle of Man

Record Repositories and Libraries

The General Registry, Finch Road, Douglas, Isle of Man (free leaflets available setting out the scope of the records held; sent on receipt of SAE)
The Manx Museum, Crellin's Hill, Douglas, Isle of Man (holds microfilm copies of some documents)
Isle of Man Family History Society, c/o Miss P. Killip, 9 Sandringham Drive, Onchan, Isle of Man
Transactions of the Isle of Man Natural History & Antiquarian Society

Family Histories

BARLOW, E. A., *Quote of Qualtroughs* (privately published in New Zealand)
RADCLIFFE, CONSTANCE, *The Family of Radcliffe*

Monumental Inscriptions

FELTHAM, J. and WRIGHT, E. (ed. W. Harrison), *Memorial of God's Acre, being monumental inscriptions in the Isle of Man* (1868)

Surnames

MOORE, A. W. *Manx Names* (2nd edn. 1903)

Kent

The Kent Bibliography, Including Genealogical Records (The Library Association, London and Home Counties Branch), 1977

Record Repositories and Libraries

Kent County Archives Office, County Hall, Maidstone
Kent Archives Office, Public Library, Folkestone

Kent Archives Office, Public Library, Ramsgate

Maidstone Museum, St Faith's Street, Maidstone

Maidstone Public Library, St Faith's Street, Maidstone (also houses library of the Kent Archaeological Society)

Cathedral Library and City Record Office, The Precincts, Canterbury

Institute of Genealogical and Heraldic Studies, Northgate, Canterbury

Rochester Diocesan Registry and Cathedral Library, c/o Messrs. Arnold Tuff & Grunwade, The Precincts, Rochester

HULL, F., *Guide to the Kent Archives Office, Maidstone* (Kent County Council, 1958); 1st Supplement 1957-68 (1971); 2nd Supplement 1969-80 (1982)

HULL, F., *Handlist of Kent County Council Records 1889-1945* (1972)

HULL, F. (ed.), *Calendar of the White and Black Books of the Cinque Ports, 1432-1955* (Kent Archaeological Society Records Publication, vol. 19)

HUSSEY, A. (ed.), *Kent Obit and Lamp Rents* (Kent Archaeological Society Records Publication, vol. 14)

DU BOULAY, F. R. H. (ed.), *Documents Illustrative of Medieval Kentish Society* (Kent Archaeological Society Record Publication, vol. 18, 1964)

COTTON, C. (ed.), *A Kentish Cartulary of the Order of St John of Jerusalem* (Kent Archaeological Society Records Publication, vol. 11, 1930)

General reference can be made to *Archaeologia Cantiana*, issued annually since 1858 by the Kent Archaeological Society

Directories

BERGESS, WINIFRED F., and RIDDELL, BARBARA R.M., *Kent Directories Located* (Kent County Council, 2nd edn. 1973)

Episcopal Registers and Records of Clergy

Canterbury registers are extant from 1279, except 1327-49 and 1636-60

Rochester registers are extant from 1319, except 1467-93

The *Canterbury and York Society* has published the following registers from Canterbury:

Registrum Johannis Pechani (vol. 55, 1908); also published as Registrum epistolarum fratis Johannis Peckham, ed. C.T. MARTIN, *Rolls Series* (vol. 77, 1882-5)

GRAHAM, R., (ed.), Registrum Roberti Winchelsey (vols. 51, 52, 1952, 1956)

FRERE, W.H., (ed.) Registrum Matthei Parker (vols. 35, 36, 39, 1928-33)

JACOB, E.F., (ed.) The register of Henry Chichele (vols. 42, 45-7, 1937-47)

JOHNSON, C., (ed.) Registrum Hamonis Hethe (vols. 48, 49, 1948)

DUNKIN, E.H.W., *Index to the Act Books of the Archbishops of Canterbury, 1663-1859; extended and edited by C. Jenkins and E.A. Fry (British Record Society Index Library*, vols. 55, 63, 1929, 1938)

FRAMPTON, T.S., 'Early presentations to Kent benefices' (*Archaeologica Cantiana*, vol. 20, 1893)

WOODRUFF, C.E., and CHURCHILL, I.J., (eds.), 'Calendar of Institutions by the Chapter of Canterbury, sede vacante' (*Kent Archaeological Society Records Branch*, publication no. 8, 1923)

FIELDING, C.H., *The Records of Rochester* (1910)

JENKINS, C., 'Cardinal Morton's Register' (in *Tudor Studies*, ed. R.W. Seton-Watson, 1924)

LE NEVE, JOHN, (ed.), *Fasti Ecclesiae Anglicanae: Canterbury, Rochester, and Winchester Diocese 1541-1857*, 1715, corrected and continued to 1854 by T. Duffus Hardy (3 vols., 1854)

Feet of Fines

JOHN, RICHARD I., 'Pedes Finium' (*Arch. Cant.*, vols. 1-6, 1858-1865)

GREENSTREET, J., 'Abstract of Kent Fines levied in the reign of Edward II' (*Arch. Cant.*, vols. 11, 15, 1877, 1883)

GREENSTREET, J., 'Abstract of Feet of Fines for Kent temp. Edward III' (*Arch. Cant.*, vols. 18, 20, 1889, 1893)

GRIFFIN, RALPH (ed.), *Calendar of Kent Feet of Fines to the end of the Reign of Henry III* (issued in four parts; Kent Archaeological Records Publication, vol. 15)

Freemen

COWPER, J.M., *Roll of Freemen of the City of Canterbury from A.D. 1392-1800* (1903)

Heraldry

HUMPHERY-SMITH, C., *Heraldry in Canterbury Cathedral* (1975)

SUMMERS, PETER, *Hatchments in Britain, vol. 5: Kent, Surrey, Sussex* (1985)

Inquisitiones Post Mortem

'Inquisitiones Post Mortem, 1235-7' (*Arch. Cant.*, vols. 2-6, 1859-65)

Manorial Records

Manorial Society Publication. Kentish Manorial Incidents. A.12

Marriage Licences

COWPER, J.M., *Canterbury Marriage Licences, series 1-6, 1568-1750* (1892-1906)

WILLIS, A.J., *Canterbury Marriage Licences: vol. 1, 1751-80* (1967)

WILLIS, A.J., *Canterbury Marriage Licences: vol. 2, 1781-1809* (1969)

WILLIS, A.J., *Canterbury Marriage Licences: vol. 3, 1810-37* (1971)
WILLIS, A.J., *Canterbury Licences General, 1568-1646* (1972)

Members of Parliament

CAVE-BROWN, J., 'Knights of the shire for Kent, A.D. 1275-1831' (*Arch. Cant.*, vol. 21, 1895)
SMITH, F.F., *Rochester in Parliament, 1295-1933: including the Chatham and Gillingham Divisions* (1933)
WILKS, G., *Barons of the Cinque Ports* (1893)

Monumental Inscriptions

DUNCAN, L.L., *Monumental Inscriptions in All Saints Churchyard, Lydd* (1927)

Parochial and Non-Parochial Registers

BUCKLAND, W.E., 'The Parish Registers and Records in the Diocese of Rochester' (*K.A.S.*, vol. 1, 1912)
MURRAY, K. M. E. (ed.), *Register of Daniel Rough, Common Clerk of Romney, 1353-1380* (Kent Archaeological Society Records Publication, vol. 16, 1946)
WOODRUFF, C.E., *Inventory of Parish Registers and other Records in the [Canterbury] diocese* (1922)
PALGRAVE-MOORE, PATRICK (ed.), *National Index of Parish Registers: vol. IV, Kent, Surrey and Sussex* (1980)
PALGRAVE-MOORE, PATRICK (ed.), *Parish Registers and Transcripts in the Kent County Record Office* (1981)

Pedigrees

BERRY, W., *County Genealogies: pedigrees of the families in the County of Kent* (1837)

School Registers

HART, W.G., (ed.), *Register of Tonbridge School, 1553-1820* (1935)

Subsidies

ARNOLD, A.A., 'Poll Tax in Rochester, September 1660' (*Arch. Cant.*, vol. 30, 1914)

Visitations

BANNERMAN, W.B., (ed.), 'Visitation of Kent, 1530' (*Harleian Society*, vol. 74, 1923)

BANNERMAN, W.B., (ed.), 'Visitation of Kent, 1574' (*H.S.*, vol. 75, 1925)
BANNERMAN, W.B., (ed.), 'Visitation of Kent, 1592' (*H.S.*, vol. 75, 1925)
HOVENDEN, R., (ed.), 'Visitation of Kent, 1619-21' (*H.S.*, vol. 42, 1878)
ARMYTAGE, G., (ed.), 'Visitation of Kent, 1663-8' (*H.S.*, vol. 54, 1906)

Wills and Administrations

PLOMER, H.R., (ed.), 'Index of wills and administrations...in the Probate
Registry at Canterbury, 1396-1558 and 1640-50' (*British Record Society Index
Library*, vol. 50, 1920)
RIDGE, C.H., (ed.), 'Index of wills and administrations...at Canterbury,
1558-77: administrations only 1539-45' (*British Record Society Index Library*, vol.
65, 1940)
WOODRUFF, C.E., (ed.), 'Sede Vacante wills, 1278-1559' (*K.A.S. Records
Branch*, publication no. 3, 1914)
DUNCAN, I.L., (ed.), 'Index of Wills proved in the Rochester Consistory
Court, 1440-1561' (*K.A.S. Records Branch*, publication no. 9, 1924)
SMITH, C.C., (ed.), *Index of Wills proved in the Prerogative Court of Canterbury: vol. 4,
1584-1604* (1901)
CARVER, A. and PLOMER, H.R., (eds.), *Genealogical abstracts from 16th century
wills in the Consistory Court of Canterbury* (1929)

Lancashire

Record Repositories and Libraries

Lancashire Record Office, Bow Lane, Preston PR1 8ND
Liverpool Record Office, Brown Library, William Brown Street, Liverpool L3
8EW
Manchester Central Library, St Peter's Square, Manchester M2 5DP
John Rylands Library, University of Manchester, Oxford Road, Manchester
M13 9PP
Wigan Central Library, Local History and Archives Department, Rodney
Street, Wigan
Greater Manchester Record Office, County Hal, Piccadilly Gardens, Manches-
ter M60 3HP
Bolton Metropolitan Borough Archives, Central Library, Le Mans Crescent,
Bolton BL1 1SA
Stockport Local Studies Library, Central Library, Wellington Road South,
Stockport SK13 9RS
Wigan Record Office, Town Hall, Leigh WN7 2DY
FRANCE, R.S., *Guide to the Lancashire Record Office* (Lancashire County Council,
1962)

Ecclesiastical Records and Records of Clergy

RAINES, F.R., and BAILEY, J.E.,'The Rectors of Manchester and Wardens of the Collegiate Church of that Town' (*Chetham Society*, 2nd ser., vols. 5, 6, 1885)

BROWN-BILL, J., (ed.), 'The Coucher Book of Furness Abbey' (*Chetham Society*, 2nd ser., vol. 26, 1892)

WEBB, A.N., (ed.), 'An edition of the Cartulary of Burscough Abbey' (*Chetham Society*, 3rd ser., vol. 18, 1970)

Feet of Fines

FARRER, W., (ed.), 'Feet of Fines for Lancashire 1196-1558' (*Lancashire and Cheshire Record Society*, vols. 39, 46, 50, 16, 1899-1910)

Heraldry

SUMMERS, PETER, *Hatchments in Britain: vol. 3, the Northern Counties* (1980)

Inquisitiones Post Mortem

HARPER, R.J., (ed.), *Ducatus Lancastriensis Inquisitiones Post Mortem: vol. 1, Edward I–Charles I* (London Record Commissioners, 1823)

LANGTON, W., (ed.), 'Abstracts of the Inquistiones Post Mortem made by Christopher Townley and Roger Dodsworth [Richard I–Elizabeth I]' (*Chetham Society*, 1st ser., vol. 95, 1875)

STOKES, E., 'Calendar of the Duchy of Lancaster Inquisitiones Post Mortem, Edward I–Henry VII' (*Genealogical Magazine*, vols. 2-6, 1899-1902)

RYLANDS, J.P., (ed.), 'Lancashire Inquistiones Post Mortem: Stuart Period' (*L.C.R.S.*, vols. 3, 16, 17, 1880, 1887, 1888)

Manorial Documents

BAILEY, J.E., and LYONS, P., 'Two Compoti of the Lancashire and Cheshire Manors of Henry de Lacy, Earl of Lincoln 1294-6 and 1304-5' (*Chetham Society*, 1st ser., vol. 112, 1884)

Members of Parliament and Office Holders

PINK, W.D., and BEAVEN, A.B., *The Parliamentary Representation of Lancashire, 1258-1885* (1896)

HORNYOLD-STRICKLAND, H., 'Biographical Sketches of the Members of Parliament for Lancashire' (*Chetham Society*, n.s. vol. 93, 1935)

ROSKELL, J.S., 'The Knights of the Shire for the County Palatine of Lancaster, 1377-1460' (*Chetham Society*, n.s. vol. 96, 1937)

SOMERVILLE, SIR ROBERT, *Office Holders in the Duchy of Lancaster from 1603* (1972)

Parochial and Non-Parochial Registers

BULMER, J.A., *Unitarian Chapel, Cairo Street, Warrington: Births and Christenings 1724-1853; Deaths and Burials, 1788-1960; Monumental Inscriptions, 1749-1969* (1981)

PEET, H., (ed.), 'The earliest registers of the parish of Liverpool...with an appendix, being a report on the ecclesiastical records in the Diocese of Liverpool' (*Lancashire Parish Record Society*, 1909)

SMITH, J.P., *Genealogist's Atlas of Lancashire with list of Parish Registers* (1930)

LEONARD, K., (ed.), *Register of Births, Baptisms, Deaths, and Burials 1788-1812 and Baptisms and Burials 1813-1837 in the parish of Hawkshead, Lancashire* (1971)

Publications of the *Lancashire Parish Register Society*, 1898 onwards

Pedigrees

FOSTER, J., *Pedigrees of the County Families of Lancashire* (1873)

Quarter Sessions

TAIT, J., (ed.), Lancashire Quarter Sessions records, vol. I, Quarter session rolls 1590-1606 (Chetham Society, n.s. vol. 77, 1914)

AXON, E., (ed.), Manchester Sessions, notes of proceedings before Oswald Mosley (1616-1630), Nicholas Mosley (1661-1672) and Sir Oswald Mosley (1734-1739) and other magistrates, vol. I, 1616-1622/3 (only volume published)

Subsidies

EARWAKER, J.P., (ed.), 'Lancashire Subsidies for 1541, 1622, 1628' (*L.C.R.S.*, vol. 12, 1885)

VINCENT, J.A.C., (ed.), 'Lancashire Subsidies for 1216-1307' (*L.C.R.S.*, vol. 27, 1893)

RYLANDS, J.P., (ed.), 'The Lancashire Subsidy for 1332' (*L.C.R.S.*, vol. 31, 1896)

TAIT, J., (ed.), 'Taxation in the Salford Hundred, 1524-1802' (L.S.n.s.83, 1924)

Surnames

MCKINLEY, R.A., (ed.), *The English Surnames Series:vol. 4, Lancashire* (1982)

Visitations

LANGTON, W., (ed.), 'Visitation of Lancashire, 1533' (Chetham Society o.s., vols. 98, 110, 1876, 1882)

RAINES, F.R., (ed.), 'Visitation of Lancashire, 1567' (C.S. o.s., vol. 81, 1870)

RAINES, F.R., (ed.), 'Visitation of Lancashire, 1613' (C.S. o.s., vol. 82, 1871)

RAINES, F.R., (ed.), 'Visitation of Lancashire, 1664-5' (C.S. o.s., vols. 84-5, 88, 1872, 1873)

Wills and Administrations

FISHWICK, H., (ed.), 'Lancashire Wills proved at Richmond, 1457-1680' (*L.C.R.S.*, vols. 10, 13, 23, 66, 1884-1913)

Leicestershire

Record Repositories and Libraries

Leicestershire Record Office, 57 New Walk, Leicester LE1 7JB
Leicester Museums Department of Archives, The Museum and Art Gallery, New Walk, Leicester

Episcopal Registers and Records of Clergy

For bishop's registers, *see* Lincolnshire
'Leicestershire Livings in the Reign of James I' (*Association of Architectural Societies*, vol. 29)
'Subsidies of the Clergy in the Archdeaconry of Leicester in the 17th century' (*Assoc. Archit. Socs.*, vol. 27)

Freemen

HARTOPP, H., (ed.), *Registers of the Freemen of Leicester: vol. 1, 1196-1770* (1927)

Inquisitiones Post Mortem

FLETCHER, W.G.D., 'Notes on Leicestershire Inquisitiones Post Mortem' (*Transactions of the Leicestershire Architectural and Archaeological Society*, vol. 6, 1884)

Manorial Records

FARNHAM, G.F., et al, *Leicestershire Manorial Records* (1919-22)
FARNHAM, G.F., *Leicester Medieval Village Notes* (6 vols., 1929-33)
THOMPSON, A.H., *Leicestershire Manorial Researches of George Farnham* (1930)

Marriage Licences

HARTOPP, H., (ed.), 'Leicestershire Marriage Licences, 1570-1729' (*British Record Society Index Library*, vol. 38, 1910)

Parochial and Non-Parochial Registers

FOSTER, C.W., *Leicestershire Parish Registers: Index to Bishops' Transcripts in the Registry of the Archdeaconry of Leicestershire, 1561-1700, and a List of Leicestershire Parish Registers prior to 1890 by Henry Hartopp* (1909)

Pedigrees

FARNHAM, G.F., *Leicestershire Medieval Pedigrees* (1925)

Urban Records

CHINNERY, G.A., (ed.), *Records of the Borough of Leicester*: vol. V, 1689-1835, Hall Books and Papers; vol. VI, 1689-1835, Chamberlain's Accounts; vol. VII, 1689-1835, Judicial and Allied Records

Visitations

NICHOLS, J., *History and Antiquities of the County of Leicester* (first published 1792-1811, repr. 1971), contains the visitations for 1563, 1619 and 1682-3 and an index of Pedigrees in vol. 1, pt. ii.
FETHERSTON, J., (ed.), 'Visitation of Leicestershire in 1619' (*Harleian Society*, vol. 2, 1870)

Wills and Administrations

HARTOPP, H., 'Wills proved in the Court of the Archdeaconry of Leicestershire, 1495-1750' (*British Record Society Index Library*, vols. 27, 51, 1902, 1920)

Lincolnshire

Record Repositories and Libraries

Lincolnshire Archives Office, The Castle, Lincoln LN1 3AB
Grimsby Borough Archives Office, Town Clerk's Office, Municipal Offices,
Town Hall Square, Grimsby
Lincoln Public Library, Free School Lane, Lincoln

Directories

WHITE, W., *History, Gazetteer and Directory of Lincolnshire and the City and Diocese of Lincoln* (repr. of 1856 edn., 1978)

Episcopal Registers and Records of Clergy

Lincoln registers are extant from 1209 with some gaps
The *Canterbury and York Society* and the *Lincoln Record Society* have jointly published the following registers:
Hugh de Welles 1209-35 (vols. 1, 3, 4, 1907-8)
Robert Grosseteste 1235-53; Henry de Lexington 1254-8 (vol. 10, 1913)
Richard Gravesend 1258-79 (vol. 31, 1925)
Oliver Sutton, 1280-99 (vol. 39, 1948)
FOSTER, C.W., (ed.), 'Lincoln Episcopal Records...1571-84' (*Canterbury and York Society*, vol. 11, 1913)
FOSTER, C.W., (ed.), 'The State of the Church in the Reigns of Elizabeth and James I, as illustrated by documents relating to the Diocese of Lincoln: vol. 1' (no more published: *Lincoln Record Society*, vol. 23, 1926)
FOSTER, C.W., (ed.), 'Institutions to Benefices in the Diocese of Lincoln, 1540-70' (*Association of Architectural Societies*, vols. 24-5
FOSTER, C.W., (ed.), 'Admissions to Benefices in the Diocese of Lincoln, 1587-1660' (*A.A.S.*, vol. 39)
FOSTER, C.W., (ed.), 'The Lincoln Episcopal Registers' (*A.A.S.*, vol. 41)
FOSTER, W.E., *Plundered Ministers of Lincolnshire, with Notes* (1900)
GIBBONS, A., (ed.), *Liber Antiquus de Ordinationibus Vicariarum, 1209-35* (1888)
THOMPSON, A.H., 'Notes on Pluralists in the Diocese of Lincoln in 1336' (*A.A.S.*, vol. 33)
MAJOR, K., 'Lincoln Diocesan Records' (reprinted from *Transactions of the Royal Historical Society*, 4th series, vol. 22, 1940)
GREENAWAY, D.E. (ed.), *Fasti Ecclesiae Anglicanae: Diocese of Lincoln, 1066-1300* (1977)
KING, H.P.F. (ed.), *Fasti Ecclesiae Anglicanae: Diocese of Lincoln, 1300-1541* (1962)

Feet of Fines

MASSINGBERD, W.O., (ed.), *Lincolnshire Records: Abstracts of Final Concords, 1193-1244* (1896)

FOSTER, C.W., (ed.), 'Final Concords...1244-72, with additions 1176-1250' (*L.R.S.*, vol. 17, 1920)

Inquisitiones Post Mortem

'Lincolnshire Inquisitiones Post Mortem, 1241-82' (*A.A.S.*, vol. 25)

Marriage Licences

GIBBONS, A., (ed.), *An abstract of the Allegation Books preserved in the Registry of the Bishop of Lincoln, 1598-1628* (1888)
'Lincolnshire Marriage Bonds' (*Northern Genealogist*, vols. 1 and 3)

Monumental Inscriptions

EDWIN-COLE, James, 'Monumental Inscriptions at Roughton' (*The Genealogist*, vol. 7, 1883)

Members of Parliament

'Members of Parliament for Lincolnshire, 1213-1327' (*Lincolnshire Notes and Queries*, 1931)

Parochial and Non-Parochial Registers

MADDISON, A.R., (ed.), 'Lincolnshire Pedigrees' (*Harleian Society*, vols. 50, 51, 52, 55, 1902-6)

School Registers

JALLAND, R., *Free Grammar School of Queen Elizabeth in Horncastle* (1894)
GOULDING, R.W., *Some Louth Grammar School Boys of the 16th and 17th Centuries* (1925-32)

Subsidies

'List of Lincolnshire Subsidies, 1154-1672 in the Public Record Office' (*Lincs. N. & Q.*, vols. 9, 10)
SALTER, H.E., (ed.), *The Subsidy collected in the Diocese of Lincoln, 1526* (1909)

Visitations

MARSHALL, G. W. (ed.), 'Visitation of Lincolnshire in 1562-4' (*The Genealogist*, vols. 3, 4, 1879, 1880)

METCALFE, W.C., *The Visitation of the County of Lincoln, 1562-4* (1881)
MARSHALL, G. W. (ed.), 'Visitation of Lincolnshire in 1592' (*The Genealogist*, vols. 5, 6, 1881, 1882)
GREEN, E., (ed.), 'Visitation of the County of Lincoln, 1666' (*L.R.S.*, publication no. 8, 1917)
GIBBONS, A., *Notes on the Visitations of Lincolnshire* (1890-1898)

Wills and Administrations

GIBBONS, A., *Abstracts of Wills from Lincoln Episcopal Registers 1280-1547* (1888)
MADDISON, A.R., *Lincolnshire Wills: Abstracts, 1500-1617* (2 vols, 1888, 1891)
FOSTER, C.W., (ed.), 'Abstracts of wills registered in the Lincoln District Probate Registry, 1506-32' (*L.R.S.*, vols. 5, 10, 24, 1914-30)
FOSTER, C.W., (ed.), 'Calendar of Lincoln Wills 1320-1652' (*British Record Society Index Library*, vols. 28, 41, 1902, 1910)
FOSTER, C.W., (ed.), 'Calendar of Lincoln Administrations 1540-1659' (*B.R.S.I.L.*, vol. 52, 1921)
FOSTER, C.W., (ed.), 'Calendar of Lincoln Wills 1530-1699' (*B.R.S.I.L.*, vol. 57, 1930)

London and Middlesex

Record Repositories and Libraries

Baptist Historical Society and Baptist Union Library, 4 Southampton Row, WC1B 4AB
British Library, Department of Western MSS, Great Russell Street, WC1B 3DG
College of Arms, Queen Victoria Street, EC4
Corporation of London Records Office, PO Box 270, Guildhall, EC2P 2EJ
Drapers' Company, Drapers' Hall, London EC2
Duchy of Cornwall Office, 10 Buckingham Gate, SW1
General Register Office (Office of Population Censuses and Surveys), St Catherine's House, 10 Kingsway, EC2B 6JP
Greater London Record Office and History Library, 40 Northampton Road, EC1 OAB
Guildhall Library, Aldermanbury, EC2P 2EJ
House of Lords Record Office, SW1A OPW
India Office Library and Records, 197 Blackfriars Road, SE1 8NG
Inner Temple Library, Temple, London EC4
Institute of Historical Research, University of London, Senate House, Malet Street, London WC1E 7HU
Lambeth Palace Library, SE1 7JU
Leathersellers' Company, 15 St Helen's Place, EC3
Lincoln's Inn Library, WC2A 3TN

London Library, 14 St James's Square, SW1
Mercers' Company, Mercers Hall, Ironmonger Lane, EC2
Middle Temple Library, Middle Temple Lane, EC4
National Army Museum, Royal Hospital Road, SW3 4HT
The Principal Registry of the Family Division, Somerset House, Strand, WC2R
    1LP
Public Record Office, Chancery Lane, WC2A 1LR
Public Record Office, Census Search Room, Portugal Street, WC2
Public Record Office, Ruskin Avenue, Kew, Richmond, Surrey TW9 4DU
Royal Commission on Historical Manuscripts (housing the National Register
    of Archives, the Manorial Documents Register and the Tithe Documents
    Register), Quality House, Quality Court, Chancery Lane, WC2A 1HP
Skinners' Company, Skinners' Hall, 8 Dowgate, EC4R 2SP
Society of Antiquaries of London, Burlington House, Piccadilly, W1V OHS
Society of Friends Library, Friends House, Euston Road, NW1 2BJ
Society of Genealogists, 14, Charterhouse Buildings, London EC1M 7BA
Stationers' Company, Stationers' Hall, London EC4
United Reformed Church History Society, 86 Tavistock Place, WC1H 9RT
Victoria and Albert Museum Library, South Kensington, SW7 2RL
Vintners' Company, 1 Vintners' Place, Upper Thames Street, EC4V 3BE
Westminster Abbey Muniment Room and Library, SW1 3PA
Westminster City Libraries, Archive Department, Victoria Library, Bucking-
    ham Palace Road, SW1W 9UD
Westminster Diocesan Archives, Archbishop's House, Ambrosden Avenue,
    SW1
Dr Williams's Library, 14 Gordon Square, WC1H OAG

London Borough Libraries
Barnet Public Library, The Burroughs, Hendon NW4 4BE
Bromley Central Library, Bromley, Kent BR1 1EX
Camden: Hampstead Central Library, Swiss Cottage, NW3; also Holborn
    Central Library, 32-8 Theobalds Road, WC2
Croydon Public Library, Katherine Street, Croydon CR9 1ET
Hackney Libraries Department, Archives Department, Shoreditch Library,
    Pitfield Street, N1 6EX
Hammersmith Public Library Archives Department, Shepherds Bush Library,
    Uxbridge Road, W12
Haringey Libraries, Museum and Arts Department, Bruce Castle, Lordship
    Lane, N17 8NU
Hounslow: Chiswick District Library, Duke's Avenue, W4; Hounslow District
    Library, Treaty Road, Hounslow, Middlesex
Islington Central Library, 68 Holloway Road, N7 8IN
Kensington and Chelsea Central Library, Hornton Street, W8; Chelsea
    Library, Manresa Road, SW3
Lambeth Public Library, Minet Library, 52 Knatchbull Road, SE5
Lewisham Libraries Department, Archives and Local History Department, The
    Manor House, Old Road, Lee, SE13
Newham Public Libraries, Stratford Reference Library, Water Lane, E15

Southwark: Newington District Library, Walworth Road, SE17
Tower Hamlets Local History Library, Central Library, Bancroft Road, E1 4DA
Waltham Forest: Leyton Library, High Road, Leyton E10 5QH; Walthamstow
   Museum of Local History, Vestry House, Vestry Road, Walthamstow E17
Wandsworth: Battersea District Library, 265 Lavender Hill, SW11

Books
COX, J., and PADFIELD, T., *Tracing Your Ancestors in the Public Record Office*
   (1981)
JONES, P.A., *A Guide to the Records in the Guildhall Library* (1951)
SIMS, J.M., 'London and Middlesex: published records' (*London Record Society*,
   1970); see also other publications by the society
Other London Record Society publications
London Possessory Assizes, vol. 1, 1965
London Inhabitants within the walls, 1695, vol. 2, 1966
London Consistory Court Wills, 1492-1547, vol. 3, 1967
The London Eyre of 1244, Helena M. Chew and Martin Weinbaum (eds.), vol. 6,
   1970
The Port and Trade of Early Elizabethan London Documents, Brian Dietz (ed.), vol. 8,
   1972
London Assize of Nuisance, 1301-1431, A Calendar, Helena M. Chew and William
   Kellaway (eds.), vol. 10, 1973
The London Eyre of 1276, Martin Weinbaum (ed.), vol. 12, 1976
London and Middlesex Chantry Certificates, 1548, C. J. Kitching (ed.), vol. 16, 1980
Trinity House of Deptford: Transactions, 1609-35, O. G. Harris (ed.), vol. 19, 1983

Aliens

HALLEN, A.W.C., 'List of Strangers in London 1567-8' (*Genealogist's Magazine*,
   vol. 1, 1897-8)
KIRK, R.E.G., and KIRK, E.F., (eds.), 'Return of Aliens dwelling in the City
   and Suburbs of London, Henry VIII to James I' (*Huguenot Society*, publication
   10, 1900-8)

Episcopal Registers and Records of Clergy

London registers are extant from 1306, except for 1337-61, 1376-81, 1621-7 and
   1646-60.
The *Canterbury and York Society* has issued the following registers:
Ralph Baldock 1304-78 (vol. 7, 1911); Gilbert Seagrave, 1304-37 (vol. 7, 1911);
   Richard Newport, 1304-77 (vol. 7, 1911); Stephen Gravesend 1303-77 (vol. 7,
   1911); Simon of Sudbury 1362-75 (vols. 34, 38, 1927, 1938)
HENNESSY, G., *Novum Repertorium Ecclesiasticum Parochiale, or, London Diocesan
   Clergy Succession from the Earliest Times to 1898* (1898)
HENNESSY, G., 'Notes on the Ecclesiastical Registers of London' (*St Paul's
   Ecclesiastical Society*, vol. 4)

ADAMS, R.H., *The Parish Clerks of London* (1971)
GREENAWAY, D. E., *Fasti Ecclesiae Anglicanae: St Paul's, London 1066-1300* (1968)
HORN, J.M., *Fasti Ecclesiae Anglicanae: St Paul's, London 1300-1541* (1963)
HORN, J.M., *Fasti Ecclesiae Anglicanae: St Paul's, London 1541-1857* (1969)

Feet of Fines

HARDY, W.J., and PAGE, W., (eds.), *Feet of Fines of London and Middlesex, 1189-1569* (1892-3)

Freemen

'Register of Freemen temp. Hen. VIII and Edward VI' (*Transactions of the London and Middlesex Archaeological Society*)

Heraldry

BROMLEY, J., *The Armorial Bearings of the Guilds of London* (1961)
see also Cambridgeshire entry

Inquisitiones Post Mortem

PHILLIMORE, W.P.W., (ed.), *Calendar of London Inquisitiones Post Mortem, 1485-1645* (1890)
FRY, G.S., (ed.), 'Abstracts of Inquisitiones Post Mortem relating to the City of London, 1485-1603' (*British Record Society Index Library*, vols. 15, 26, 33, 1896-1908)

Manorial Records

MARCHAM, F., (ed.), 'Eton College Property in Hampstead and adjacent parishes: also court rolls of Hornsey, 1603-1701 by W. McB. Marcham' (*T.L.M.A.S.*, 1930)

Marriage Licences

ARMYTAGE, G.J., (ed.), 'Allegations for Marriage Licences, 1520-1828' (*Harleian Society*, vols. 25-6, 1887)
ARMYTAGE, G.J., (ed.), 'Allegations for Marriage Licences issued by the Dean and Chapter of Westminster, 1558-1699' (*Harleian Society*, vol. 23, 1886)
GLENCROSS, R.M., (ed.), 'Calendar of Marriage Licence Allegations, 1597-1700' (*B.R.S.I.L.*, vols. 62, 66, 1937, 1940)

Members of Parliament and Officials

BEAVEN, A.B., *Aldermen of the City of London: with notes on Parliamentary Representation, 1216-1912* (2 vols., 1908, 1913)
KINGSFORD, C. L. (ed.), *Chronicles of London* (1977 facsimile of 1905 edn.)
'Knights of the Shire for Middlesex, 1295-1832' (*T.L.M.A.S.*, n.s. vol. 5, 1864)
WOODHEAD, J.R., *The Rulers of London 1660-89* (1965)

Muster Roll

LOTT, T., 'Account of the Muster of the Citizens of London, 31 Henry VII 1540' (*Archaeologia*, vol. 32, 1847)

Parochial and Non-Parochial Registers

NEWCOURT, R., *Repertorium Ecclesiasticum Parochiale Londiniensis: An Ecclesiastical Parochial History of the Diocese of London* (2 vols., 1708, 1710)
Vestry Minutes of Parishes within the City of London (Guildhall Library, 1958)
Churchwardens' Accounts of Parishes within the City of London (Guildhall Library, 1960)
A Hand List of Parish Registers within the City of London (Guildhall Library, 1963)
A Survey of the Parish Registers of the Diocese of Southwark, Inner London Area (Greater London Record Office, 1970)
A Survey of the Parish Registers of the Diocese of London, Inner London Area (Greater London Record Office, 1968)
GRAHAM, N.H., *The Genealogist's Consolidated Guides to Parish and Nonconformist Registers*: Outer London area (1981)
GRAHAM, N.H., *The Genealogist's Consolidated Guides to Parish and Nonconformist Registers*: Inner London area (1981)

Pedigrees

ARMYTAGE, G.J., (ed.), 'Middlesex Pedigrees 1572-1634 as collected by Richard Mundy' (*Harleian Society*, vol. 65, 1914)

Place Names

FIELD, J., (ed.), *The Place Names of Greater London* (1980)
GOVER, J.E.B., MAWER, A., STENTON, F.M., and MADGE, S.J., *The English Place Name Society: vol. 18, Middlesex apart from the City of London* (1943)
KEENE, C.H., *Field Names of the London Borough of Ealing*

Protestation Roll

'The Protestation of 1641-2: London and Middlesex' (*British Archivist*, vol. 1). Contains details of those who signed the Protestation in the parishes of St

Sepulchre and St Leonard, Shoreditch; Clerkenwell; Finchley; Friern
Barnet; Hampstead; Hornsey; Islington; Stoke Newington; Willesden;
Stepney; St Leonard, Bromley; Limehouse; Poplar and Blackwall; Ratcliff;
Stratford Bow; Spitalfields; Bethnal Green; Mile End; Highgate; Edmonton;
Enfield; Hadley; South Mimms.

Quarter Sessions

JEFFERSON, J.C., (ed.), 'Middlesex County Records, 3 Edward VI-4 James II,
  1540-1688 (*Middlesex County Records Society*, 1886-92)
BOWLER, H., (ed.), 'London Sessions Records, 1605-85' (*Catholic Record Society*,
  vol. 34, 1934). Catholic entries only.
Guide to Middlesex Sessions Records (Greater London Council, 1965)

School Registers

MARSH, B., and CRISP, F.A., (eds.), *Alumni Carthusiani...1614-1872* [Charter-
  house School] (1913)
GUN, W.T.J., (ed.), *Harrow School Register, 1571-1800* (1934)
THOMPSON, W.S., (ed.), *Highgate School Roll, 1565-1922* (1927)
ROBINSON, C.J., (ed.), *Register of Scholars admitted into the Merchant Taylors' School,
  1562-1874* (1936)
HART, E.P., (ed.), *Merchant Taylors' School Register, 1561-1934* (2 vols., 1936)
SIMMONDS, M.J., (ed.), *The Merchant Taylors' School, 1561-1909* (1930)
BARKER, G.F.R., and STENNING, A.H., *Record of Old Westminsters...from earliest
  times c. 1560 to 1927* (1928)
MCDONNELL, SIR M., *The Registers of St Paul's School, London, 1509-1748* (1980)

Subsidies

WEINBAUM, M., *London unter Edvard I und II, 1293-4*
'The Lay Subsidy of 1411-12' (*British Archaeological Association*, vol. 44)

Visitations

HOWARD, J.J., and ARMYTAGE, G.J., (ed.), 'The Visitation of London, 1568'
  (*Harleian Society*, vol. 1, 1869)
RAWLINS, Sophia W. (ed.),'Visitations of London, 1568', with additional
  pedigrees 1569-90, the arms of the City Companies and a London Subsidy
  Roll 1589, edited from the transcripts prepared ad annotated by the late H.
  Stanford Landon (*H.S.*, vols. 109, 110, 1963)
HOWARD, J.J., and CHESTER, J.L., (eds.), 'The Visitation of London, 1633-5'
  (*H.S.*, vols. 15, 17, 1880, 1883)
WHITMORE, J.B., and CLARKE, A.W.H., 'London Visitation Pedigrees,
  1664' (*H.S.*, vol. 92, 1940)
FOSTER, J., (ed.), *Visitation of Middlesex, 1663* (1887)

Wills and Administrations

FITCH, Marc (ed.), 'Index to Testamentary Records in the Commissary Court of London (London Division)', vol. 1, 1374-1488 (*British Record Society Index Library*, vol. 82, 1969); vol. 2, 1489-1570 (*British Record Society Index Library*, vol. 86, 1974)

FITCH, Marc (ed.), 'Index to Testamentary Records in the Archdeaconry Court of London', vol. 1 [1363]-1649 (*British Record Society Index Library*, vol. 89, 1979)

DARLINGTON, Ida (ed.), 'London Consistory Court Wills 1492-1547' (London Record Society, Vol. I, 1967)

SHARPE, R.R., (ed.), *Calendar of Wills proved in the Court of Hustings, 1258-1688* (Corporation of the City of London, 1889-90)

Calendar of Wills and Administrations, etc., of the Commissary Court of the Dean and Chapter of Westminster 1504-1829 (H.M.S.O., 1864)

BURKE, A.M., *Indexes to Ancient Testamentary Records of Westminster, 1228-1700* (1913)

'Hampton Wills, 1374-1810' (*The Genealogist*, n.s. vols. 35-8, 1919-22)

Norfolk

Record Repositories and Libraries

Norfolk and Norwich Record Office, Central Library, Norwich NR2 1NJ

Muniment Room of the Dean and Chapter, The Cathedral, Norwich

Great Yarmouth Borough Records, Town Clerk's Department, Town Hall, Great Yarmouth

KENNEDY, J., (ed.), *Guide to Norfolk and Norwich Record Office* (1966)

PALGRAVE-MOORE, P., *The Norfolk Index: A Topographical Index of Printed and Manuscript Materials, both private and public, relating to Norfolk Genealogy* (1970)

Notes for the Assistance of Genealogists (Norfolk Record Office, 1970)

Apprenticeship Records

Yarmouth Apprenticeship Indentures 1563-1665

Censuses

PAGE, R.A.F., *Norwich Census 1851: parish of St George, Colegate* (1983)

PAGE, R.A.F., *Norwich Census, 1851: parishes of St Martin at Place and St Martin at Oak, Norfolk* (*Norfolk and Norwich Geneaogical Society*, vol. 7, 1975)

PAGE, R.A.F. and PALGRAVE-MOORE, Patrick, *Norwich Census, 1851: parishes of St Helen, Ss Simon and Jude, St Michael at Plea, St Etheldred, St Peter Hungate, St Edmund, St James* (*Norfolk and Norwich Genealogical Society*, vol. 9, 1977)
BANKOWSKY, H., *Norwich Census, 1851: parish of St Michael at Thorn* (*Norfolk and Norwich Genealogical Society*, 1984)

Directories

A History Gazetteer and Directory of Norfolk and the City and County of Norwich (reprint of 1845 edn.)

Episcopal Registers and Records of Clergy

Norwich registers are extant from 1299. Some gaps.
BASKERVILLE, G., 'Married clergy and pensioned religious in Norwich Diocese, 1555' (*English Historical Review*, vol. 43, 1933)

Feet of Fines

'Calendar of Norfolk Feet of Fines, 1191-6' (*Norfolk and Norwich Archaeological Society*, vol. 16, 1863)
RYE, W., (ed.), 'Abstracts of Feet of Fines for Norfolk, 1191-1216' (*N.&.N.A.S.*, vol. 34, 1881)
RYE, W., (ed.), *Short Calendar for Norfolk: Richard I-Edward I, 1189-1485* (2 vols., 1885, 1886)
RYE, W., (ed.), 'Index to Norfolk Feet of Fines, Henry VIII-Mary I' (*Norfolk Antiquarian Miscellany*, vol. 2)

Freemen

RYE, W., (ed.), *A Calendar of the Freemen of Great Yarmouth, 1429-1800* (*Norfolk Archaeological Society*, 1910)
RYE, W., (ed.), *A Calendar of the Freemen of King's Lynn, 1292-1836* (*Norfolk Archaeological Society*, 1913)
RYE, W., (ed.), *A Calendar of the Freemen of Norwich, 1317-1603* (1888)
MILLICAN, P., (ed.), *Freemen of Norwich, 1548-1713* (1934)
MILLICAN, P., (ed.), 'Freemen of Norwich, 1714-1752' (*Norfolk Record Society*, vol. 23, 1952)

Hearth Tax

Hearth Tax for Norfolk, 1664 (Norfolk Genealogy vol. 15, *Norfolk and Norwich Genealogical Society*, 1983)

Heraldry

FARRER, E., *Church Heraldry of Norfolk* (3 vols., 1887-93)
SUMMERS, PETER, (ed.), *Hatchments in Britain: vol. 2, Norfolk and Suffolk* (1976)

Inquisitiones Post Mortem

1216-1649: Index to Inquisitiones Post Mortem Henry III – Charles I
(1216-1649) (W.D. SELBY *Norfolk Records*, vol. 2, 1892)

Marriage Licences

RYE, W., *Index of Norfolk Marriage Licences, 1563-88* (1926)
FONE, J.F., *Norwich Marriages 1812-1837* (Norfolk Genealogy vol. 14, *Norfolk and Norwich Genealogical Society*, 1982)

Muster Rolls

'Muster Roll of the Hundred of North Greenhoe, c. 1523' (*Norfolk Record Society*, vol. 1, 1931)
'Musters for Divers Hundreds: 1569, 1572, 1574, 1577' (*Norfolk Record Society*, vols. 6 and 7, 1935, 1936)
RYE, W., 'State Papers relating to Musters, Beacons, Ship Money, etc., 1626-40' (*N.&N.A.S.*, vol. 50, 1907)

Officials

PALGRAVE-MOORE, P., *The Mayors and Lord Mayors of Norwich, 1836-1974* (1979)

Parochial and Non-Parochial Registers

PALGRAVE-MOORE, Patrick, *The Parish Registers of Norfolk: Rackheath 1645-1837* (*Norfolk and Norwich Genealogical Society*, Monograph Series, no. 1, 1984)
CARROW, C.W. and PALGRAVE-MOORE, P., *The Parish Registers of Norfolk, Bodney 1653-1839* (*Norfolk and Norwich Genealogical Society, Monograph Series*, no. 2, 1984)
SANDERSON, E.W., *Attleborough Parish Registers 1552-1840*
and *see also* Cambridgeshire entry

Pedigrees

CAMPLING, A., 'East Anglian Pedigrees' (*Harleian Society*, vol. 91, 1939; *Norfolk and Norwich Record Society*, vol. 13, 1940) RYE, W., *Norfolk Families* (1913)

PALGRAVE-MOORE, P., *Norfolk Pedigrees: parts 1-3* (Norfolk Genealogy, vols. 6, 8, 13, *Norfolk and Norwich Genealogical Society*, 1974, 1976, 1983)

Quarter Sessions

'Norfolk Quarter Sessions Roll, 1394-7' (*Norfolk Record Society*, vol. 8, 1936)
HOWELL, JAMES D.E., 'Norfolk Quarter Sessions Order Book, 1650-7' (*Norfolk Record Society*, vol. 26, 1955)

Surnames

MCKINLEY, R.A., (ed.), *English Surnames Series: vol. 2, Norfolk and Suffolk Surnames in the Middle Ages* (1975)

Visitations

DASHWOOD, G.H., (ed.), 'The Visitation of Norfolk, 1563' (*N.&.N.A.S.*, vol. 7-12, 1878-95)
RYE, W., (ed.), 'The Visitation of Norfolk, 1563' (*Harleian Society*, vol. 32, 1891)
CLARKE, A.W.H., (ed.), 'The Visitation of Norfolk, 1664' (*Harleian Society*, vols. 85, 86, 1933, 1934) (also published by *Norfolk Record Society*, vols. 4, 5, 1934)

Wills and Administrations

FARROW, M.A., (ed.), 'Index to Wills proved in the Consistory Court of Norwich, 1370-1550' (*British Record Society Index Library*, vol. 69, 1945)
FARROW, M.A., (ed.), 'Index to Wills proved in the Consistory Court of Norwich, 1550-1603' (*British Record Society Index Library*, vol. 73, 1950)
PALGRAVE-MOORE, P., *Index to Wills proved in the Norfolk Archdeaconry Court, 1453-1542, 1542-1560, 1560-1603/4* (Norfolk Genealogy, vols. 3, 5 and 10, *Norfolk and Norwich Genealogical Society* 1971, 1973, 1978)
FARROW, M.A. and BARTON, T.F., *Index of Wills Proved in the Consistory Court of Norwich, 1004-1686* (*Norfolk Record Society*, vol 25, 1958)
BARTON, T.F. and FARROW, M.A., *Index of Wills proved in the Consistory Court of Norwich, 1687-1750* (*Norfolk Record Society*, vol. 34, 1965)
BARTON, T.F., FARROW, M.A. and BEDINGFIELD, A.L., *Index of Wills Proved in the Consistory Court of Norwich, 1751-1818* (*Norfolk Record Society*, vol. 38, 1969)

Northamptonshire

Record Repositories and Libraries

Northamptonshire Record Office, Delapré Abbey, Northampton
Northampton Central Library, Abington Street, Northampton
KING, P.I., (ed.), *Summary Guide to the Northamptonshire Record Office* (1954)

Episcopal Registers and Records of Clergy

Peterborough registers extant from 1541

LONGDEN, H.I., *Northamptonshire and Rutland Clergy from 1500* (15 vols. in 5, 1938-42)

Index volume published by Northamptonshire Record Society, 1952 MEL-LOWS, W.T., 'The Last Days of Peterborough Monastery' (*Northamptonshire Record Society*, vol. 12, 1947)

Family Histories

JEFFS, L.D., *Jeffs Families of Northamptonshire* (1973)

FINCH, M.E., 'The Wealth of Five Northamptonshire Families 1540-1640' (*N.R.S.*, vol. 19, 1956)

Heraldry

SUMMERS, PETER, (ed.), *Hatchments in Britain: vol. 1, Northants., Warwicks., Worcs.* (1974)

Manorial Records

PAGE, FRANCES M., (ed.), 'Wellingborough Manorial Accounts, 1258-1323' (*N.R.S.*, vol. 8, 1936)

BROOKE, C.N.L., and POSTAN, M., 'Carte Nativorum: A Peterborough Cartulary of the 14th Century' (*N.R.S.*, vol. 20, 1960)

Musters

WAKE, J., 'Copy of papers relating to musters, beacons, subsidies, etc., 1586-1623' (*Northampton Record Society*, vol. 3, 1926)

WAKE, J., (ed.), 'Montagu Musters Book, 1602-23' (*N.R.S.*, vol. 7, 1935)

GORING, J.J., and WAKE, J., 'Northamptonshire Lieutenancy Papers and other Documents 1580-1614' (*N.R.S.*, vol. 27, 1975)

HATLEY, V.A., 'Northamptonshire Militia Lists 1777' (*N.R.S.*, vol. 25, 1973)

Parochial and Non-Parochial Registers

ELLIOTT, H., 'The Parish Registers of Northampton and the neighbourhood' (*Association of Architectural Societies*, vol. 6)

Quarter Sessions

WAKE, J., (ed.), 'Quarter Sessions Records, 1630, 1657-8' (*N.R.S.*, vol. 1, 1924)

Pedigrees

BARRON, O., *Northamptonshire Families* (1906)

Place Names

GOVER, J.E.B., MAWER, A., and STENTON, F.M., (eds.), *The English Place Name Society: vol. 10, Northamptonshire* (1933)

Subsidies

WAKE, Joan, *Muster, Beacons and Subsidies in the County of Northamptonshire, 1586-1623* (*Northampton Record Society*, vol. 3, 1926)

Visitations

METCALFE, W.C., (ed.), *Visitation of Northamptonshire, 1564* (1887)
METCALFE, W.C., (ed.), *Visitation of Northamptonshire, 1618/19* (1887)
LONGDEN, H.I., (ed.), *Visitation of Northamptonshire, 1681* (*Harleian Society*, vol. 87, 1935)

Wills and Administrations

PHILLIMORE, W.P.W., (ed.), 'A Calendar of Wills related to the Counties of Northamptonshire and Rutland, 1510-1652' (*British Record Society Index Library*, vol. 1, 1888)
LONGDEN, H.I., 'Administrations of the Archdeaconry of Northampton, 1516-1676' (*Miscellanea Genealogica et Heraldica*, supp. to 5th series, vols. 9 & 10, 1938)
DRUCKER, L., (ed.), 'Administrations in the Archdeaconry of Northampton, 1677-1710' (*B.R.S.I.L.*, vol. 70, 1947)
BAGGOT, Clair (ed.),'Administrations in the Archdeaconry of Northampton, 1710-1800' (*B.R.S.I.L.*, vol. 92, 1980)

Northumberland

Record Repositories and Libraries

Northumberland Record Office, Melton Park, North Gosforth, Newcastle-upon-Tyne
City Archives Office, 7 Saville Place, Newcastle-upon-Tyne

Newcastle-upon-Tyne Central Library, New Bridge Street, Newcastle-upon-Tyne
Genealogical Sources List (Northumberland Record Office)

Feet of Fines

OLIVER, A.M., and JOHNSON, C., (eds.), 'Feet of Fines, 1196-1278: Northumberland and Durham' (*Newcastle-upon-Tyne Records Committee Publications*, vol. 10, 1931)
JOHNSON, C., (ed.), 'Feet of Fines, 1272-1376: Northumberland' (*N.R.C.*, vol. 11, 1932)

Freemen

DODDS, M.H., (ed.), 'Register of Freemen of Newcastle-upon-Tyne, 1409-1710' (*N.R.C.*, vol. 3, 1923)
OLIVER, A.M., (ed.), 'Register of Freemen of Newcastle-upon-Tyne, c.1700' (*N.R.C.*, vol. 6, 1926)

Heraldry

BLAIR, C.H., 'Armorials of Northumberland: an Index and Ordinary to 1666' (*Archaeologia Aeliana*, Society of Newcastle-upon-Tyne, 3rd ser., vol. 6, 1919)
SUMMERS, PETER, (ed.), *Hatchments in Britain: vol. 3, the Northern Counties* (1980)

Inquisitiones Post Mortem

'Index to Inquisitiones Post Mortem' (*Proceedings of the Society of Antiquaries of Newcastle-upon-Tyne*, 3rd series, vol. 2)

Members of Parliament

DODDS, M.H., et al., 'Members of Parliament for Northumberland, 1258-1831' (*Archaeologia Aeliana*, 4th series, vols. 10-13, 1933-5)

Muster Rolls

RICHARDSON, G.B., (ed.), *A Muster of the Fencible Inhabitants of Newcastle, 1539* (1852)
'Muster roll of Northumberland, 1538' (*Archaeologia Aeliana*, Society of Antiquaries of Newcastle-Upon-Tyne, 5th series, vol. 3, 1975)

and Peculiar of Southwell 1588-1754' (*British Record Society Index Library*, vol. 58, 1930) Vol. 2, 'Archdeaconry Court 1701-1753, Peculiar of Southwell, 1755-1853 (*British Record Society Index Library*, vol. 60, 1935)
The following volumes are published by the Nottinghamshire Family History Society:
vol. 11: Marriages Index, Arnold Parish 1546-1837
vol. 23: Nottingham (St Mary, St Peter and St Nicholas), Part 1, Males, A-F
vol. 23: Part 2, Males, G-N
vol. 23: Part 3, Males O-Z
vol. 24: Part 4, Females
vol. 31: Newark area

Monumental Inscriptions

The following volumes are published by the Nottinghamshire Family History Society:
vol. 1: Granby, Redmile and Hickling
vol. 2: Barton-in-Fabis, Clifton and Cropwell Bishop
vol. 6: Colston Bassett, Edwalton and Scarrington
vol. 12: East Bridgford, Keyworth, Kneeton, North Clifton, North Muskham, Orston, Plumtree, South Clifton
vol. 13: East Leake, East Leake (Baptist), Rempstone, St Peter-in-the-Rushes Rempstone, Sandiacre (Derbyshire), South Muskham, West Leake
vol. 15: Whatton-in-the-Vale, Wilford, Willoughby-on-the-Wolds, Wymeswold
vol. 18: Bestwood, Blyth, Bulcote, Burton Joyce, Cromwell, Loudham
vol. 19: Nuthall, South Scarle, Stapleford, Strelley, Tollerton, Wysall

Muster Rolls

'Muster Roll of 1595, Newark Ward' (*Transactions of the Thoroton Society*, vol. 10, 1914)

Parochial and Non-Parochial Registers

BLAGG, M., (ed.), '17th century Parish Register transcripts belonging to the Peculiar of Southwell' (*Thoroton Society Record Series*, vol. 1, 1903)

Pedigrees

PHILLIMORE, W.P.W., *County Pedigrees: vol. 1, Nottinghamshire* (1910)

Place Names

GOVER, J.E.B., MAWER, A., and STENTON, F.M., (eds.), *The English Place Name Society, vol. 17, Nottinghamshire* (1940)

Poll Books

READ, MYRTLE J., *Poll Books of Nottingham and Nottinghamshire, 1710* (1958)

Quarter Sessions

COPNALL, H.H., *Nottinghamshire County Records of the 17th century* (1915)
STEVENSON, W.H., et al., *Records of the Borough of Nottingham, 1155-1760* (7 vols., 1882-1914)

Visitations

LONGSTAFFE, W.H.D., (ed.), 'Visitation of Nottinghamshire, 1530' (*Surtees Society*, vol. 41, 1863)
MARSHALL, G.W., (ed.), 'Visitations of Nottinghamshire, 1569, 1615' (*Harleian Society*, vol. 4, 1871)
TRAIN. K., 'Nottinghamshire Visitation 1662-1664' (*Thoroton Society Record Series*, vol. 13, 1950)

Wills and Administrations

see also LEACH, A.F., (ed.), 'Visitations and Memorials of Southwell Minster, 1470-1541' (*Camden Society*, n.s. vol. 48, 1891)
'Nottinghamshire Funeral Certificates, 1627-39' (*The Genealogist*, vol. 7, 1883)
CLAY, J.W., (ed.), 'North Country Wills: Nottingham, 1383-1604' (*Surtees Society*, vols. 116, 121, 1908, 1912)

Oxfordshire

Record Repositories and Libraries

Oxfordshire County Record Office, County Hall, New Road, Oxford OX1 1ND
Department of Western Manuscripts, Bodleian Library, Broad Street, Oxford OX1 3BG: amongst many other items of interest, houses the University of Oxford's archives
The various university colleges all house their own collections of archives, many of which relate to their property holdings in different parts of the country
CORDEAUX, E.H., and MERRY, D.M., *A Bibliography of Printed Works relating to Oxfordshire* (1955)
Summary Catalogue of Privately Deposited Records in the Oxfordshire County Record Office (1966)

Beginning your Oxfordshire Family Tree (Oxfordshire Family History Society, 1978)
HAMS, COLIN G., *The Oxfordshire Genealogical Section on the open shelves in the Bodleian Library (Seldon End)*
STEER, FRANCIS W., (ed.), *The Archives of New College, Oxford* (1974)
DRENNAN, B. St. G., *Keble College Centenary Register* (1970)
JONES, J., *A Catalogue of the Archives of Balliol College, Oxford* (1984)

Deeds

HASSALL, W.O., *Index of Persons in Oxfordshire Deeds Acquired by the Bodleian Library 1878-1963*

Episcopal Registers and Records of Clergy

Oxford registers are extant from 1541
PHILIP, I.G., 'Diocesan Records in the Bodleian Library' (*Genealogist's Magazine*, vol. 8, 1938/9)

Family Histories

WILDER, W.C., *The Wilder Family: The Wilders of Ipsden, Oxfordshire* (1944)

Feet of Fines

SALTER, H.E., 'Feet of Fines for Oxfordshire, 1995-1292' (*Oxfordshire Record Society*, vol. 12, 1930)

Hearth Tax

WEINSTOCK, M.M.B., (ed.), *Hearth Tax Returns for Oxfordshire, 1665*

Heraldry

SUMMERS, PETER, (ed.), *Hatchments in Britain: vol. 4, Bucks., Beds., Berks., Wilts., Oxon.* (1983)

Marriage Registers

BLACKMORE, (ed.), *An Index of Oxford Diocesan Marriage Bonds, 1661-1860 , in the Bodleian Library* (typescript)
GIBSON, J.S.W., *The Oxfordshire Marriage Index 1537-1837*

Phillimore Marriage Registers for Oxfordshire, all to 1837
    vol. 1, 1909: Chipping Norton, Pyrton, Wootton,
    vol. 2, 1910: Cassington, Eynsham, Harnborough, Northmoor, Standlake,
    Stanton Harcourt, Yarnton

Members of Parliament

WILLIAMS, W.R., *Parliamentary History of Oxford, 1213-1899* (1899)

Muster Rolls and Military Records

TOYNBEE, M., and YOUNG, P., *Strangers in Oxford: Royalist Lodgings in St Aldates, in 1643* (1973)

Parochial and Non-Parochial Registers

HAMS, COLIN G., *Oxfordshire Parish Registers deposited originals and transcripts- first supplement*
STEEL, D.J., et al (ed.), *National Index of Parish Registers, vol. 5: The South Midlands and the Welsh Borders* (1966, reprinted 1976)
DAVIS, F.N., (trans.) 'The Parochial Collections of Anthony à Wood and Richard Rawlinson' (*Oxfordshire Record Society*, vols. 2, 4, 11, 1920-9)

Pedigrees

WILLOUGHBY, G., and GYLL, J., *Pedigrees of the Counties of Wiltshire and Oxfordshire*

Place Names

GELLING, MARGARET (ed.), *The English Place Name Society, vols. 23, 24, Oxfordshire* Parts 1 and 2 (based on material collected by D. M. Stenton) (1953, 1956)

Quarter Sessions

Calendar of Oxfordshire Quarter Sessions Records, 1687-1830

Subsidies

SALTER, H.E., (ed.), 'Surveys and tokens, including subsidies, 1543-4, 1648, 1667' (*Oxford Historical Society*, vol. 75, 1923)

Surnames

MCKINLEY, R.A., (ed.), *The English Surnames Series: vol. 3, Oxfordshire* (1978)

Visitations

TURNER, W.H., (ed.), 'Visitations of Oxfordshire, 1566, 1574, 1634' (*Harleian Society*, vol. 5, 1871)

Wills and Administrations

BARRAT, D. M., *Probate Records of the Courts of the Bishop and Archdeacon of Oxford, 1516-1732* vol. 1, A to K (British Record Society Index Library, vol. 92, 1981)
GRIFFITHS, J., *Index of Wills, etc., proved in the Court of the Chancellor of Oxford, 1436-1814* (8 vols., 1862)
'Some Oxfordshire Wills, 1393-1510' (*Oxfordshire Record Society*, vol. 39, 1958)
GIBSON, S., 'Abstracts from Wills and Testamentary Documents of Binders, Printers and Stationers of Oxford, 1493-1638' (*Bibliographical Society*, 1907)

Rutland

Lay Subsidy Rolls

CORNALL, J. (ed.), *Tudor Rutland: The County Community under Henry VIII* (Lay Subsidy Roll of 1574-5 and also the Military Survey of 1552) (*Rutland Record Society*, vol. 1, 1980)
ARMYTAGE, G.J., (ed.), 'The Visitation of Rutland, 1618-19' (*Harleian Society*, vol. 3, 1870)
RYLANDS, W.H., (ed.), 'The Visitation of Rutland, 1681-2' (*Harleian Society*, vol. 73, 1922)

Wills and Administrations

PHILLIMORE, W.P.W., (ed.), 'Calendar of Wills relating to Rutland, 1510-1652' (*British Record Society Index Library*, vol. 1, 1888)

Shropshire

Record Repositories and Libraries

Salop Record Office, New Shirehall, Abbey Foregate, Shrewsbury SY2 6ND
Shrewsbury Borough Archives, Guildhall, Dogpole, Shrewsbury

Shrewsbury Borough Library, Castle Gates, Shrewsbury
A Guide to Shropshire Records, Shrewsbury (Shropshire County Council, 1952)

Episcopal Registers and Records of Clergy

See Herefordshire, Staffordshire
'Institutions of Shropshire Incumbents' (*Transactions of the Shropshire Archaeological Society*, 3rd series, vols. 1, 5, 8; 4th series, vol. 2, 1901, 1905, 1908)

Feet of Fines

'Feet of Fines for Shropshire, 1196-1218' (*T.S.A.S.*, 1st series, vols. 4, 6, 1881, 1883; 2nd series, vol. 10, 1898; 3rd series, vols. 6, 9, 1906, 1909)

Inquisitiones Post Mortem

'Shropshire Inquisitiones Post Mortem, 1254-1383' (*T.S.A.S.*, 2nd series, vol. 11, 1899)
FLETCHER, W.G.D., (ed.), *Shropshire Inquisitiones Post Mortem, Henry III–Charles I (1245-1645)* (1926 reprint from *T.S.A.S.*)

Muster Roll

'Shropshire Muster Rolls 1532-40' (*T.S.A.S.*, 3rd series, vols. 8, 9, 17, 20, 1908, 1909)

Parochial and Non-Parochial Registers

PEELE, E.C., and CLEASE, R.S., *Shropshire Parish Documents* (Shropshire County Council, 1896)
see also Gloucestershire entry

Quarter Sessions

Abstracts of the Orders made by the Court of Quarter Sessions for Shropshire, 1638- (13 vols., Shropshire County Record Office, 1889)

School Registers

CALVERT, E., (ed.), *Shrewsbury School: Registrum Scolarium, 1562-1635* (1892)

Subsidies

'Shropshire returns for the Subsidy of 1327' (*T.S.A.S.*, 2nd series, vols. 1, 4, 5,
   11, 1889, 1892, 1893, 1899; 3rd series, vols. 5, 7, 1905, 1907)
'Shropshire returns for the Subsidy of 1641' (*T.S.A.S.*, 3rd series, vol. 4, 1904)

Visitations

GRAZEBROOK, G., and RYLANDS, J.P., (eds.), 'Visitation of Shropshire,
   1623' (*Harleian Society*, vols. 28, 29, 1889)

Wills and Administrations

MATTHEWS, G. F. *Shropshire Probates in the Prerogative Court of Canterbury,
   1700-1749* (privately published 1929)
TRINDER, BARRIE and COX, JEFF, (eds.), *Yeomen and Colliers in Telford* (1980)

Somerset

Record Repositories and Libraries

Somerset Record Office, Obridge Road, Taunton TA2 7PU
Victoria Art Gallery and Municipal Libraries, Bridge Street, Bath
Library of the Somerset Archaeological and Natural History Society and Local
   Studies Library, Taunton Castle, Taunton

Episcopal Records and Records of Clergy

Bath & Wells registers are extant from 1265 except from 1267-1309, 1364-1401,
   1444-92, 1548-53 and 1626-9.
The *Somerset Record Society* has issued the following printed registers:
   Walter Gifford 1265-6; Henry Bowett 1401-7; vol. 13, 1899
   John Drokensford 1309-27, vol. 1, 1887
   Ralph de Salopia 1329-63, vols. 9, 10, 1895, 1896
   Nicholas Bubwith 1407-24, vols. 29, 30, 1913, 1914
   John Stafford 1425-43, vols. 31, 32, 1915, 1916
   Thomas Bekynton 1443-65, vols. 49, 50, 1934, 1935
BATTEN, E.C., (ed.), *Register of Richard Fox, Bishop of Bath and Wells 1492-94*
   (1889)
WEAVER, F.W., *Somerset Incumbents 1300-1750 from the Hugo MSS in the British
   Museum* (1889)

HOLMES, T.S., *Report to Convocation on the Ecclesiastical Records of the Diocese of Bath and Wells* (1914)
JONES, B., (ed.), *Fasti Ecclesiae Anglicanae: Bath and Wells Diocese 1300-1541* (1964)
HORN, J.M., and BAILEY, D.S., (eds.), *Fasti Ecclesiae Anglicanae: Bath and Wells Diocese 1541-1857* (1979)

Family Histories

BURDEN, JOY, *Winging Westward: A History of Kingweston House and the Dickinson Family* (1974)

Feet of Fines

GREEN, E., (ed.), 'Abstracts of Pedes Finium for Somerset, 1196-1485' (*Somerset Record Society*, vols. 6, 12, 17, 22, 1892-1906)

Inquisitiones Post Mortem

'Abstracts of Somerset Inquisitiones Post Mortem for the reign of Henry III' (*Collectanea Topographica et Genealogica*, vol. 2, 1835)
'Calendar of Somerset Inquisitiones Post Mortem, 1216-1485' (*Transactions of the Somerset Archaeological and Natural History Society*, vol. 44)

Monumental Inscriptions

'Monumental Inscriptions of Road' (*The Genealogist*, vol. 5, 1881)

Muster Rolls

GREEN, E., (ed.), 'Certificate of the Somerset Musters, 1569' (*S.R.S.*, vol. 20, 1904)

Parochial and Non-Parochial Registers

JEWERS, A.J., (ed.), *Bishops' Transcripts at Wells* (5 vols., 1913-19)
KING, J.E., *Inventory of Parochial Documents in the Diocese of Bath and Wells* (1938)
'Somerset Non-Parochial Registers' (*T.S.A.N.H.S.*, vol. 79)
STEVENS-COX, G., (ed.), *The Early Church Registers (christenings, marriages and burials) of Long Ashton (1558-1600)*
CARTER, R.W., *Parish Surveys in Somerset: Whitestaunton* (1981)

Quarter Sessions

BATES, E.H., (ed.) 'Somerset Quarter Sessions, 1607-77' (*S.R.S.*, vols. 23, 24, 28, 34, 1907-19)

Subsidies

DICKINSON, F.H., 'Kirby's Quest for Somerset, 1348-9' (*S.R.S.*, vol. 3, 1889)
DWELLY, E., (ed.), *Somerset Subsidies, 1624-74* (1932)

Visitations

WEAVER, F.W., (ed.), *Visitations of the County of Somerset, 1531, 1573, 1591* (1885)
COLBY, F.T., 'Visitation of Somerset, 1623' (*Harleian Society*, vol. 11, 1870)

Wills and Administrations

FRY, E.A., (ed.), 'Calendar of Wills in Taunton Archdeaconry Court
   1537-1799' (*British Record Society Index Library*, vol. 45, 1912)
FRY, E.A., (ed.), 'Calendar of Administrations in Taunton Archdeaconry Court
   1596-1799' (*B.R.S.I.L.*, vol. 53, 1922)
'Abstracts of Wells Wills, 1539-1541' (*T.S.A.N.H.S.*, vol. 41)
SHILTON, D.O., (ed.), 'Medieval Wills from Wells, 1543-1556' (*S.R.S.*, vol. 40,
   1925)
RAWLINS, S.W., (ed.), 'Somerset Wills from Exeter, 1529-1600' (*S.R.S.*, vol.
   62, 1952)

Staffordshire

Record Repositories and Libraries

Staffordshire Record Office, County Buildings, Eastgate Street, Stafford ST16
   2LZ
Lichfield Joint Record Office, Public Library, Bird Street, Lichfield WS13 6PN
Lichfield Diocesan Record Office, The Close, Lichfield
William Salt Library, 19 Eastgate Street, Stafford
University Library, University of Keele, Keele
Workers Educational Association, North Staffordshire District, Cartwright
   House, Broad Street, Henley, Stoke on Trent

Chancery Proceedings

WROTTESLEY, G., 'Early Staffordshire Chancery Proceedings, 1377-1509'
   (*William Salt Archaelogical Society*, n.s. vol. 7, 1904)
BOYD, W.K., 'Staffordshire Chancery Proceedings temp. Elizabeth I, 1560-79'
   (*W.S.A.S.*, n.s. vol. 9, 1906; 3rd series, 1926 (1928), 1931 (1933), 1938)

Episcopal Registers and Records of Clergy

Lichfield registers are extant from 1297, except for 1580-1618, 1632-61, 1671-92, 1717-49.

'Register of Roger de Norbury, Bishop of Lichfield 1322-58' (*W.S.A.S.*, vol. 1, 1880)

'Registers of Robert de Stretton, Bishop of Lichfield 1358-85' (*W.S.A.S.*, n.s. vols. 8, 10(ii), 1906, 1907)

HUTCHINSON, S.W., *The Archdeaconry of Stoke on Trent* (1893). Contains lists of incumbents, etc.

LANDOR, W.N., 'Staffordshire Incumbents and Parochial Records, 1530-1680' (*W.S.A.S.*, 3rd series, vol. 6, 1915)

COX, J.C., 'An Elizabethan Clergy List of the Diocese of Lichfield' (*Derbyshire Archaeological Society*, vol. 6, 1884)

JONES, B., (ed.), *Fasti Ecclesiae Anglicanae: Coventry and Lichfield Diocese 1300-1541* (1965)

ROBINSON, David (ed.), *Visitations of the Archdeaconry of Stafford 1829-41* (*Staffordshire Record Society*, 4th series, vol. 10, 1980)

Guide to Diocesan, Probate and Church Commissioners' Records (Lichfield Joint Record Office)

Feet of Fines

WROTTESLEY, G., (ed.), 'Staffordshire Feet of Fines, 1196-1625' (*W.S.A.S.*, vol. 3 et seq., 1883 onwards)

WEDGEWOOD, J., (ed.), 'Staffordshire Feet of Fines, 1223-1366' (*W.S.A.S.*, 3rd series, vols. 2, 4, 1911, 1913)

Members of Parliament

WEDGEWOOD, J.C., 'Staffordshire Parliamentary History from the earliest times, 1213-1841' (*W.S.A.S.*, 3rd series, 1917 (1919), 1920, 1922, 1934, 1935 (1936))

Muster Rolls

BOYD, W., 'Staffordshire Muster Roll for 1539' (*W.S.A.S.*, n.s. vols. 4-6, 1901-3)

WROTTESLEY, G., 'Staffordshire Muster Roll for 1640' (*W.S.A.S.*, vol. 15, 1894)

Parochial and Non-Parochial Registers

DONALDSON, Barbara, 'The Registration of dissenting Chapels and Meeting houses in Staffordshire 1689-1852 extracted from the return of the General

Registration Office made under te Protest and Dissenters Act 1852' (*S.A.S.*, 4th series, vol. 3, 1960

PALGRAVE-MOORE, PATRICK (ed.), *National Index of Parish Registers: vol. 6 The North Midlands, Part 1, Staffordshire* (1983)

The *Staffordshire Parish Register Society* has published the following volumes:

The Registers of All Saints, Madeley, Staffordshire: Baptisms and Burials 1775-1812

The Registers of St Michael and All Angels, Adbaston, Staffordshire: part 1, Baptisms, Marriages and Burials 1600-1726/7: part 2, Baptisms, Marriages and Burials 1727-1839

The Registers of St Mary the Virgin, High Offley, Staffordshire: Baptisms, Marriages and Burials 1659-1812

The Registers of St James the Great, Audley, Staffordshire: Baptisms, Marriages and Burials 1538-1712

The Registers of St John the Evangelist, Hanley, Staffordshire: Baptisms 1789-1803

The Registers of Wednesfield, Staffordshire: Baptisms and Burials 1751-1837

Pedigrees

CARTER, W.F., 'Notes on Staffordshire Families' (*W.S.A.S.*, 3rd series, 1910, 1925, 1927)

POLLARD, WILLIAM, *The County of Stafford and many of its Family Records* (1897)

Quarter Sessions

BURNE, S.A.H., (ed.), 'Staffordshire Quarter Sessions, 1581-1602' (*W.S.A.S.*, 3rd series, 1929 (1931), 1930 (1932), 1933 (1934), 1934 (1935), 1935 (1936)

School Registers

THOMAS, H.R., and RYAN, J., *Wolverhampton Grammar School Register, 1515-1920* (1927)

Visitations

GRAZEBROOK, H.S., (ed.), 'Heraldic Visitations of Staffordshire: 1583' (*W.S.A.S.*, vol. 3(ii), 1883)

GRAZEBROOK, H.S., (ed.), 'Heraldic Visitations of Staffordshire: 1614, 1663/4' (*W.S.A.S.*, vol. 5(ii), 1885)

ARMYTAGE, G.J., and RYLANDS, W.H., (eds.), 'Visitation of Staffordshire, 1663/4' (*Harleian Society*, vol. 63, 1912)

Wills and Administrations

PHILLIMORE, W.P.W., (ed.), 'Lichfield Wills and Administrations, 1516-1652' (*British Record Society Index Library*, vol. 7, 1892)

'Register of Stafford and Local Wills, 1537-83' (*W.S.A.S.*, 3rd series, vol. 16, 1926 (1928))

Suffolk

Record Repositories and Libraries

Suffolk Record Office (Bury St Edmunds branch), School Hall Street, Bury St Edmunds IP33 1RX
Suffolk Record Office (Ipswich branch), County Hall, Ipswich IP4 2JS
Both branches have published *Guides to Genealogical Sources*

Directories

WHITE, W., *A History, Gazetteer and Directory of Suffolk and the Towns near its borders* (1978 reprint of 1884 edn.)

Episcopal Registers and Records of Clergy

HOLMES, C., (ed.), *The Suffolk Committees for Scandalous Ministers, 1644-6* (*Suffolk Record Society*, vol. 13, 1970)
THOMPSON, R.M., (ed.), *The Archives of the Abbey of Bury St Edmunds* (1980)

Feet of Fines

RYE, W., (ed.), 'Calendar of Feet of Fines for Suffolk, 1189-1485' (*Journal of the Suffolk Institute of Archaeology*, 1900)

Heraldry

CORDER, JOAN, *Dictionary of Suffolk Arms* (1966)
CORDER, H., *A Suffolk Armory* (1968)
SUMMERS, PETER, (ed.), *Hatchments in Britain: vol. 2, Norfolk and Suffolk* (1976)

Manorial Records

COPINGER, W.A., *The Manors of Suffolk: Notes on their History with a General Index to the Holders* (7 vols., 1905-11)

Parochial and Non-Parochial Registers

REDSTONE, V.B., 'Records of Sudbury Archdeaconry: Calendar of Parish Register Transcripts' (*J.S.I.A.*, vol. 11)
see also Cambridgeshire entry

Pedigrees

MUSKETT, J.T., and JOHNSON, F., *Suffolk Manorial Families* (3 vols., 1894-1914)
GATFIELD, G., 'Index to Davy's Suffolk Collections' (*The Genealogist*, n.s. vols. 5 and 6, 1888, 1889). An index to a collection of Suffolk pedigrees made by D.E.Davy and now in the British Library.

School Registers

HERVEY, S.H.A., *Biographical List of Boys educated at King Edward VI Free Grammar School, Bury St Edmunds, 1550-1900* (1908)

Ship Money Lists

REDSTONE, V.B., 'Suffolk Ship Money Lists, 1639-40' (*J.S.I.A.*, 1904)

Subsidies

1327, 1524, 1568, 1674 (Suffolk Green Books, vols. 9, 10, 12) *See also* POWELL, E., *The Peasants' Revolt in East Anglia* (1896), details of those listed in the 1381 Poll Tax.

Surnames

MCKINLEY, R.A., (ed.), *The English Surnames Series: vol. 2, Norfolk and Suffolk in the Middle Ages* (1975)

Visitations

METCALFE, W.C., (ed.), *Visitations of Suffolk, 1561, 1577, 1612* (1882)
RYLANDS, W.H., (ed.), 'Visitation of Suffolk, 1664-8' (*Harleian Society*, vol. 61, 1910)

Wills and Administrations

REDSTONE, V.B., *Calendar of Pre-Reformation Wills, 1354-1535* (1907)
CRISP, F.A., (ed.), 'Calendar of Wills at Ipswich, 1444-1600' GANDY, W., (ed.), 'Calendar of Wills at Ipswich, 1751-93' COOKE, C.W. and R., (eds.),

'Suffolk Wills in the Prerogative Court of Canterbury, 1383-1604'
'Suffolk Wills in the Prerogative Court of Canterbury, 1444-1620' (*East Anglian*, n.s. vols. 1, 2, 3)
SERJEANT, W.R. and R.K. (eds.), 'Index to probate records of the court of the Archdeacon of Suffolk 1444-1700' vol. 1, A-K, vol. 2, L-Z (*British Record Society Index Library*, vols. 90 and 91, 1979 and 1980)

Surrey

Record Repositories and Libraries

Surrey Record Office, County Hall, Penrhyn Road, Kingston-upon-Thames KT1 2ON
Guildford Muniment Room (Surrey Record Office), Castle Arch, Guildford GU1 3SX (also houses library of the Surrey Archaeological Society)
In addition the journal *Surrey History* (published by Phillimore & Co. Ltd. for the Surrey Local History Council) sometimes contains material of interest to the genealogist

Borough Records

POWELL, D.L., 'Surrey Borough Records' (*Surrey Record Society*, vol. 29, 1929)

Feet of Fines

LEWIS, F.B., (ed.), 'Calendar of Surrey Feet of Fines, 1189-1485' (*Surrey Archaeological Society Collections*, extra vol., 1894)

Heraldry

see Kent entry

Manorial Records

POWELL, D.L., 'List of Surrey Court Rolls, with some notes of other manorial records' (*S.R.S.*, vol. 28, 1928)

Marriage Licences

BAX, A.R., *Marriage and other Licences in the Commissary Court of Surrey* (1893)

Members of Parliament

SMITH, J.E., *The Parliamentary Representation of Surrey, 1290-1924* (1927)

Muster Rolls

CRAIB, T., (ed.) 'The Surrey Muster Rolls of 1544-1684' (*S.R.S.*, vols. 2, 8, 10, 11, 1914-20)
'Surrey Muster Rolls, 1588-1626' (*S.A.C.*, vol. 30, 1922)

Parochial and Non-Parochial Registers

POWELL, D.L., 'Surrey Parish Records, Civil and Ecclesiastical' (*S.R.S.*, vol. 26, 1927)
PALGRAVE-MOORE, PATRICK, (ed.), *National Index of Parish Registers: vol. 4, Kent, Surrey and Sussex* (1980)

Pedigrees

BERRY, W., *County Genealogies: pedigrees of the Families in the County of Surrey* (1837)

Place Names

GOVER, J.E.B., MAWER, A., and STENTON, F.M., (eds.), *The English Place Name Society, vol. 11, Surrey* (1934)

School Registers

ARROWSMITH, R.L., (ed.), *Charterhouse Register, 1769-1872* (1975)

Subsidies

'The Subsidy of 1332' (*S.A.S.C.*, vol. 41, 1933)
'The Subsidy of 1593/4' (*S.A.S.C.*, vols. 18, 19, 1926, 1927)
WILLARD, J.F., and JOHNSON, H.C., (eds.), 'Surrey Taxation Returns, 1332-1623' (*S.R.S.*, vols. 18, 33, 1922, 1932)

Visitations

BANNERMAN, W.B., 'Visitations of Surrey, 1530, 1572, 1623' (*Harleian Society*, vol. 43, 1899)

ARMYTAGE, G.J., (ed.), 'Visitation of Surrey, 1662/8' (*Harleian Society*, vol. 60, 1910)

Wills and Administrations

'Wills proved in the Archdeaconry Court of Surrey, 1484-1608' (*S.R.S.*, vols. 3, 7, 15, 17, 1915-22)

Sussex

Record Repositories and Libraries

West Sussex Record Office, John Edes House, West Street, Chichester PO19 1RN

East Sussex Record Office, The Maltings, Castle Precincts, Lewes BN7 1YT

Sussex Archaeological Trust, Barbican House, Lewes

Hastings Public Museum, John's Place, Cambridge Road, Hastings

STEER, F.W., 'A Catalogue of the Earl Marshal's Papers at Arundel Castle' (*Harleian Society*, vols. 115-16, 1963-4)

WILKINSON, P.M., *A Genealogist's Guide to the West Sussex Record Office* (1981)

LESLIE, K.C., *Roots of America: An Anthology of Documents relating to American History in the West Sussex Record Office* (1977)

STEER, F.W., and VENABLES, J.E.A., (eds.), *The Goodwood Estate Archives* (vol. 1, 1970, vol. 2, 1972)

MCCANN, T.J., (ed.), *The Goodwood Estate Archives* (vol. 3, forthcoming)

STEER, F.W., and OSBORNE, N.H., (eds.), *Petworth House Archives* (vol. 1, 1968)

MCCANN, ALISON, (ed.), *Petworth House Archives* (vol. 2, 1979)

STEER, F.W., (ed.), *Arundel Castle Archives* (vol. 1; vol. 2, 1972; vol. 3, 1976; vol. 4, 1980)

STEER, F.W., (ed.), *Lavington Estate Archives* (1964)

BOOKER, J.M.L., (ed.), *The Wiston Archives* (vol. 1, 1975)

FREETH, S., (ed.), *The Wiston Archives* (vol. 2)

Diaries and Journals

BLENCOWE, R., and LOWER, M.A., (eds.), *The Diary of a Georgian Shopkeeper: Thomas Turner of East Hoathly* (1979)

NEALE, KENNETH, (ed.), *Victorian Horsham: the Diary of Henry Michell 1809-1874* (1975)

'The Journal of Giles Moore of Horsted Keynes 1656-1679' (*S.R.S.*, vol. 68, 1971)

Episcopal Registers and Records of Clergy

Chichester registers extant from 1397, except 1416-38; 1446-78
The *Sussex Record Society* has issued English abstracts of the registers of:
  Reade, Robert 1397-1415 (vols. 8 and 11, 1908, 1910)
  Praty, Richard 1438-45 (vol. 4, 1905)
HENNESSY, G., *Chichester Diocese Clergy Lists or Clergy Successions from the Earliest Times to 1900* (1900, supplement 1901)
WALCOTT, M.E.C., 'Medieval Registers of the Bishops of Chichester, with a Calendar of the Episcopal Registers' (*Transactions of the Royal Society of Literature*, 2nd series, vol. 9)
WALCOTT, M.E.C., 'Early presentations to Sussex incumbencies' (*Sussex Archaeological Collections*, vol. 17, 1865)
DUNKIN, E.H.W., 'Admissions to Sussex Benefices during the Commonwealth' (*S.A.C.*, vol. 33, 1883)
SAWYER, F.E., 'Crown presentations to Sussex Benefices, temp. Charles II' (*S.A.C.*, vol. 35, 1887)
SAWYER, F.E., 'Proceedings of the Sussex Committee of Plundered Ministers' (*S.A.C.*, vols. 30, 31, 32, 36, 1880-2, 1887)
REDWOOD, B.C., and WILSON, A.E., (eds.), 'Custumals of the Sussex Manors of the Archbishops of Canterbury' (*Sussex Record Society*, vol. 57, 1958)
PECKHAM, W.D., (ed.), 'Acts of the Dean and Chapter of Chichester, 1545-1642' (*S.R.S.*, vol. 58, 1959)
HORN, J.M., (ed.), *Fasti Ecclesiae Anglicanae: Chichester Diocese 1300-1541* (1964)
HORN, J.M., (ed.), *Fasti Ecclesiae Anglicanae: Chichester Diocese 1541-1857* (revised edn. 1971)
STEER, F.W., and KIRBY, I.M., (eds.), *A Catalogue of the Records of the Bishop, Archdeacons and former Exempt Jurisdictions* (1966)

Family Histories

CHILD, K., *Some account of the Child Family 1550-1861* (1973)
BOOKER, J.M.L., (ed.),*The Clough and Butler Archives* (1965)
GILL, P., (ed.) *The Cobden and Unwin Papers* (1967)
GLADWISH, V.E.R., *The Rape of Hastings Family of Gladwishe 1225-1980* (1981)
OSBORNE, N.H., (ed.), *The Lytton Manuscripts* (1967)
PARRY, ANN, *The Carylls of Harting* (1976)
READMAN, A.E., (ed.), *The Buckle Papers* (1981)
RIDGE, DUDLEY, *A Sussex Family: The Family of Ridge from 1500 to the Present Day* (1975)
STEER, F.W., (ed.), *The Mitford Archives* (2 vols., 1961, 1970)
VOLK, CONRAD, *Magnus Volk of Brighton* (1971)
WAGNER, SIR ANTHONY, and DALE, ANTONY, *The Wagners of Brighton* (1983)

Feet of Fines

SALZMAN, L.F., (ed.), 'Feet of Fines for Sussex, 1190-1509' (*S.R.S.*, vols. 1, 7, 23, 1903-16)

Heraldry

HUMPHERY-SMITH, C.R., *A Sussex Armory* (1975)
LAMBARDE, F., 'Coats of Arms in Sussex Churches' (*S.A.C.*, vols. 67-76, 000-0000)
HUXFORD, J.F., *Arms of Sussex Families* (1981)
SUMMERS, PETER, (ed.), *Hatchments in Britain: vol. 5, Kent, Surrey and Sussex* (1985)

Inquisitiones Post Mortem

ATTREE, F.W.R., (ed.), 'Sussex Inquisitiones Post Mortem 1485-1649' (*S.R.S.*, vol. 14, 1912)
SALZMAN, L.F., (ed.), 'Calendar of Sussex Inquisitiones Post Mortem 1558-83'(*S.R.S.*, vol. 3, 1904)
HOLGATE, M.S., (ed.), 'Abstracts of Sussex Inquisitiones Post Mortem 1541-1616' (*S.R.S.*, vol. 33, 1927)
ATTREE, F.W.R., 'Sussex Inquisitiones Post Mortem temp. Hen. VII, Jas. I, Chas. I' (*S.A.C.*, vol. 52, 1909)

Marriage Licences

DUNKIN, E.H.W., (ed.), 'Lewes Marriage Licences 1586-1643' (*S.R.S.*, vol. 1, 1902)
SHORT, B., *The Geography of Local Migration and Marriage in Sussex 1500-1900* (1983)

Members of Parliament

COOPER, W., *A Parliamentary History of Sussex, 1295-1832* (1834)
ALBERY, W., *A Parliamentary History of Horsham, 1295-1885* (1927)
BRENT, COLIN, *Lewes Parliamentary Borough in 1871: a household and political directory* (1978)

Parochial and Non-Parochial Registers

RENSHAW, W.C., 'Bishops' Transcripts for the Archdeaconry of Lewes' (*S.A.C.*, vol. 55, 1912)

CHALLEN, W.H., 'Sussex entries in London parish registers' (*Sussex Notes and Queries*, vols. 1-6, 1926-1932)
PALGRAVE-MOORE, PATRICK, (ed.), *National Index of Parish Registers: vol. 4, Kent, Surrey and Sussex* (1981)

Pedigrees

BERRY, W., *County Genealogies: pedigrees of the Families in the County of Sussex* (1830)
COMBER, J., *Sussex Genealogies* (1931)

Place Names

GOVER, J.E.B., MAWER, A., and STENTON, F.M., (eds.), *The English Place Name Society*, vols. *6 and 7, Sussex* (1969 reprint)

Poor Law Records

COLEMAN, J.M., *Sussex Poor Law Records: a Catalogue* (1960)

Quarter Sessions Records

Descriptive Report on the Quarter Sessions and the Official and Ecclesiastical Records in the Custody of the East and West Sussex County Councils (1954)

Shipping Records

'Rye Shipping Records 1566-1590' (*S.R.S.*, vol. 64, 1966)

Subsidies

NOYES, T.H., 'Roll of a Subsidy levied 13 Henry IV, 1411-12' (*S.A.C.*, vol. 10, 1858)
HILDSON, W., (ed.), 'Sussex Subsidies 1296, 1327, 1322' (*S.R.S.*, vol. 10, 1910)
CORNWALL, J., 'The Lay Subsidy Rolls for the County of Sussex, 1524-5' (*S.R.S.*, vol. 56, 1956)

Urban Records

'Common Council of Chichester, 1783-1826' (*S.R.S.*, vol. 62)
'Lewes Town Book, 1542-1701' (*S.R.S.*, vol. 48, 1947)
'Lewes Town Book, 1702-1837' (*S.R.S.*, vol. 69, 1973)
'Lewes Town Book, 1837-1901' (*S.R.S.*, vol. 70, 1976)

Visitations

BANNERMAN, W.B., (ed.), 'Visitations of Sussex, 1530, 1633-4' (*Harleian Society*, vol. 53, 1905)
PHILLIPS, T., (ed.), *Visitation of Sussex, 1570* (1840)
CLARKE, A.W.H., (ed.), 'Visitation of Sussex, 1662' (*H.S.*, vol. 89, 1937)

Wills and Administrations

BURCHALL, M.J., *A Guide to Sussex Probate Records* (1981)
FRY, E.A., (ed.), 'Chichester Consistory Wills, 1482-1800' (*British Record Society Index Library*, vol. 49, 1915)
HALL, W.H., (ed.), 'Sussex Wills at Lewes, 1541-1652' (*British Record Society Index Library*, vol. 24, 1901)
'Some Sussex *sede vacante* wills' (*Sussex Notes and Queries*, vol. 6, *c*.1932)
'Sussex Wills in the Public Record Office and the British Museum' (*S.N.Q.*, vol. 6, 1932)
FRY, E.A., (ed.), 'Chichester Consistory Administrations 1555-1800' (*British Record Society Index Library*, vol. 64, 1940)
RICHE, R.G., (ed.), 'Sussex Wills' (*S.R.S.*, vols. 41-3, 45, 1935-41)
MCCANN, T.J., (ed.), *West Sussex Probate Inventories 1521-1834: a Catalogue* (microfiche, 1981)

Warwickshire

Record Repositories and Libraries

Warwickshire County Record Office, Priory Park, Cape Road, Warwick CV34 4JS
Birmingham City Library, Ratcliff Place, Birmingham
The Main Library, University of Birmingham, Edgbaston, Birmingham
Coventry City Record Office, 9 Kay Lane, Coventry
Shakespeare's Birthplace Trust Record Office, Guild Street, Stratford-upon-Avon CV37 6QW
RATCLIFF, S.S., and JOHNSON, H.C., *Warwickshire County Records* (Warwickshire County Council Records Committee, 1935)
TIBBITTS, E.G., *Ancient Records of Warwick* (1938)
The *Birmingham and Midlands Society for Genealogy and Heraldry* has published the following volumes:
Midland Genealogical Directory 1978 (1978)
Midland Genealogical Directory Supplement no. 1 (1981)
MARKWELL, F.G., *Tracing your Ancestors in Warwickshire* (1981)

Ecclesiastical Records and Records of Clergy

JONES, B., (ed.), *Fasti Ecclesiae Anglicanae: Coventry and Lichfield Diocese 1300-1541* (1964)

Family Histories

CHURCH, R.A., *Kenricks in Hardware: a Warwickshire Family Business 1791-1966* (1969)

Feet of Fines

WELLSTOOD, F.C., et al, (eds.), 'Abstracts of Warwickshire Feet of Fines, 1195-1509' (*Dugdale Society*, vols. 11, 15, 18, 1932-43)

Heraldry

SUMMERS, PETER, (ed.), *Hatchments in Britain: vol. 1, Northamptonshire, Warwickshire, Worcestershire* (1974)

Muster Roll

BLOOM, J.H., (ed.), *Warwickshire Muster Roll of 1599* (1905)

Parochial Records

The Registers of St George, Hockley, Warwickshire: Baptisms and Burials, 1858, Marriages 1830-7 (*Birmingham and Midland Society for Genealogy and Heraldry Publication*, 1980)

The Registers of St Giles, Sheldon, Warwickshire: Baptisms 1683-1839, Marriages 1684-1858, Burials 1683-1841 (*Birmingham and Midland Society for Genealogy and Heraldry Publications*, ca.1982)

Birmingham and Midland Society for Genealogy and Heraldry – Parish Registers: Birmingham, Cathedral church, Marriages 1715-1800 (n.d., c.1982); Coventry, St Michael's, Baptisms, Marriages and Burials 1662-1742 (1983); Elmdon, Marriages, Burials and Baptisms 1742-1846 (1981); Wasperton, St John the Baptist, Baptisms, Marriages and Burials 1538-1837 (1982)

see also Gloucestershire entry

Place Names

GOVER, J.E.B., MAWER, F.A., and STENTON, F.M., with HOUGHTON, F.G.S., (eds.), *The English Place Name Society, vol. 13, Warwickshire* (1936)

Quarter Sessions

RATCLIFF, S.C., and JOHNSON, H.C., (eds.), *Quarter Sessions Order Book,
1625-50* (2 vols., Warwickshire County Council Record Committee, 1935-6)
KIMBALL, E.G., (ed.), 'Rolls of the Warwickshire and Coventry Sessions of the
Peace, 1347-77' (*Dugdale Society*, vol. 16, 1939)

Subsidies

WELLSTOOD, F.C., 'Subsidy of 1333' (*Dugdale Society*, vol. 6, 1926)

Visitations

FETHERSTON, J., (ed.), 'Visitation of Warwickshire, 1619' (*Harleian Society*,
vol. 12, 1877)
RYLANDS, W.H., (ed.), 'Visitation of Warwickshire, 1682-3' (*Harleian Society*,
vol. 62, 1911)

Westmorland

Record Repositories and Libraries

Cumbria Record Office (Kendal), County Offices, Kendal

Heraldry

SUMMERS, PETER (ed.), *Hatchments in Britain: vol. 3, Northern Counties* (1980)
BOUMPHREY, R.S., HUDLESTON, C.R., and HUGHES, I., (eds.), *An
Armorial for Westmorland and Lonsdale* (1975)

Place Names

SMITH, A.H., (ed.), *The English Place Name Society, vols. 42, 43, Westmorland* (1964)

Wiltshire

Record Repositories and Libraries

Wiltshire Record Office, County Hall, Trowbridge BA14 8JG
Salisbury Diocesan Record Office, The Wren Hall, 56c, The Close, Salisbury

RATHBONE, M.G., and STEWART, P., *Guide to the Wiltshire Record Office* (2 vols., 1959, 1961)
Sources for the History of a Wiltshire Family (1981)

Episcopal Registers and Records of Clergy

Salisbury registers are extant from 1297, except for the years 1481-5, 1499-1502, 1558-60, 1584-8, 1596-8, 1645-60
The *Canterbury and York Society* has issued the register of Simon de Gandavo, 1297-1315 (vol. 40-41, 1934)
JONES, W.H., *Fasti Ecclesiae Sarisberiensis: or, a Calendar of the Bishops, Deans, Archdeacons and Members of the Cathedral Body at Salisbury* (2 vols., 1879, 1881)
PHILLIPPS, Sir THOMAS, *Institutions Clericorum in Comitatu Wiltoniae ab anno 1297 ad annum 1810* (1825)
'Wiltshire Ministers, 1643-62' (*Wiltshire Archaeological and Natural History Society*, vol. 34, 1921; *Wiltshire Notes and Queries*, vol. 8)
FLETCHER, CANON, *Incumbents of Salisbury Churches temp. the Commonwealth* (1926)
GREENAWAY, D.E., *Fasti Ecclesiae Anglicanae: Salisbury Diocese 1066-1300* (forthcoming)
HORN, J.M., *Fasti Ecclesiae Anglicanae: Salisbury Diocese 1300-1541* (1962)
GREENAWAY, D.E., *Fasti Ecclesiae Anglicanae: Salisbury Diocese 1541-1857* (forthcoming)

Family Histories

SKIDMORE, WARREN, *The Scudamores of Upton Scudamore: A Knightly Family in Medieval Wiltshire 1086-1382*

Feet of Fines

PHILLIPPS, Sir THOMAS, (ed.),*Feet of Fines for Wiltshire, 1196-1226* (1840)
PHILLIPPS, Sir THOMAS, (ed.), *Index of Feet of Fines for Wiltshire, 1327-1483* (1865)
FRY, E.A., (ed.), 'Calendar of Feet of Fines for Wiltshire, 1195-1272' (*W.A.N.H.S.*, vol. 45, 1930)
FRY, E.A., (ed.), 'Calendar of Feet of Fines for Wiltshire, Henry VIII-18 Elizabeth I' (*W.N.& Q.*, vols. 2-8)
PUGH, R.B., (ed.), 'Abstracts of Feet of Fines for Wiltshire, reigns of Edward I and Edward II' (*W.A.N.H.S. Records Branch*, vol. 1, 1939)

Heraldry

SUMMERS, PETER, (ed.), *Hatchments in Britain, vol. 4, Bedfordshire, Berkshire, Buckinghamshire, Oxfordshire, Wiltshire* (1983)

Inquisitiones Post Mortem

PHILLIPPS, Sir THOMAS, (ed.), *Wiltshire Inquisitiones Post Mortem, Henry VII-Charles I* (1866)
FRY, E.A., (ed.), 'Wiltshire Inquisitiones Post Mortem': vol. 1, Charles I;vol. 2, Henry III-Edward II; vol. 3, Edward III (*British Record Society Index Library*, vols. 23, 37, 48, 1901, 1908, 1914)

Marriage Licences

'Salisbury Marriage Licences, 1615-82' (*The Genealogist*, vols. 24, 38, 1908, 1922)
'Marriage Licences from the Court of the Dean and Chapter, Salisbury' (*W.N. & Q.*, vols. 6-8)

Muster Roll

PHILLIPPS, Sir THOMAS, (ed.), *Muster Roll for North Wiltshire, 30 Henry VIII* (1834)

Parochial and Non-Parochial Registers

COLEMAN, A., 'Lists of Non-Parochial Registers, etc.' (*W.A.N.H.S.*, vol. 27)
CARTER, B.J., *Location of Documents for Wiltshire Parishes*: 1, Aldbourne to Bromham (1981); 2, Broughton to Dinton (1981); 6, Rowe to Tilshead (1982)

Place Names

GOVER, J.E.B., MAWER, A., and STENTON, F.M., *The English Place Name Society, vol. 16, Wiltshire* (reprinted 1973)

Protestation Roll

'Wiltshire Entries on the Protestation Roll of 1641-2' (*W.N.& Q.*, vol. 7)

Ship Money

'Wiltshire and Payments of Ship Money, 1640-44' (*W.A.N.H.S.*, vol. 38, 1925)

Visitations

METCALFE, W.C., (ed.), 'Visitation of Wiltshire, 1565' (*The Genealogist*, n.s., vols. 11-13, 1894-6)
MARSHALL, G.W., (ed.), *Visitation of Wiltshire, 1623* (1882)

Wills and Administrations

'Wiltshire Wills and Administrations, etc., in the Diocesan Registry, Salisbury, 1540-1809' (*W.A.N.H.S.*, vol. 43, 1930)

Worcestershire

Record Repositories and Libraries

Worcestershire Record Office, St Helen's, Fish Street, Worcester WR1 2HN
Dudley Public Library, Steppingstone Street, Dudley
Kidderminster Public Library, Market Street, Kidderminster
Redditch Public Library, Church Road, Redditch

Episcopal Registers and Records of Clergy

Worcester registers are extant from 1268, except for 1521-2 and 1522-54
The *Worcestershire Historical Society* has printed the following registers:
    Godfrey Giffard 1268-1301 (vol. 15, 1898-1902)
    Sede vacante 1301-1435 (vol. 8, 14, 1893, 1897)
    William Gainsborough 1303-7 (vol. 22, 1907-1929)
    Thomas de Cobham 1317-27 (vol. 40, 1930)
The *Dugdale Society* has printed the following register:
    Walter Reynolds 1308-13 (vol. 9, 1894)
MILLER, G., *The Parishes of the Diocese of Worcester, with Lists of Incumbents* (2 vols., 1889, 1890)
'Worcestershire Incumbents from the Reformation to 1660' (*Worcestershire Archaeological Society*, n.s., vols. 10, 11, 1936, 1937)

Family Histories

HERBERT, M.V., *The Hickmans of Oldswinford* (1979)

Heraldry

GRAZEBROOK, H.S., *Heraldry of Worcestershire* (2 vols., 1873)
SUMMERS, PETER, (ed.), *Hatchments in Britain: vol. 1, Northamptonshire, Warwickshire, Worcestershire* (1974)

Inquisitiones Post Mortem

BUND, J.H.W., 'Worcestershire Inquisitiones Post Mortem, 1242-1326' (*W.A.S.*, vols. 2, 24, 1894, 1909)

Marriage Licences

'Worcestershire Marriage Licences 1446-1725' (*The Genealogist*, vols. 6, 7, 1882, 1883; n.s. vol. 2, 1888)

FRY, E.A., (ed.), 'Worcestershire Marriage Licences 1551-1652' (*British Record Society Index Library*, vols. 31, 39, 1904, 1910)

Members of Parliament

WILLIAMS, W.R., *The Parliamentary History of the County of Worcester, 1213-1897* (1897)

Parochial and Non-Parochial Registers

A Digest of the Parish Registers of Worcestershire prior to 1812, with a Table of the Bishops' Transcripts previous to 1700 (1899)

URWICK, WILLIAM, *Nonconformity in Worcestershire* (1897): includes a list of non-parochial registers and other records for the county.

DAY, L.G., (ed.), *The Parish Registers of Northfield, Worcestershire* (vol. 1, to 1741; vol. 2, 1742-1850)

Transcript of Registers and Historical Records of Cradley Baptist Church, Worcestershire: Baptisms and Burials 1783-1837 and other records

The Registers of Christ Church, Oldbury, Worcestershire: Baptisms and Burials (some Marriages), 1714-1812

The Registers of the Priory Church, Great Malvern, Worcestershire: vol. 1, Baptisms and Burials 1556-1708/9, Marriages 1556-1753/4; vol. 2, Baptisms and Burials 1709-1837, Marriages 1754-1837

The Church Book of the Messiah Baptist Chapel, Cinderbank, Netherton, Worcestershire: 1654-1798, including some Baptisms *The Registers of Cradley Presbyterian Church, Worcestershire*: *The Registers of St Mary, Oldswinford, Worcestershire*: vol. 1, Baptisms and Burials 1736-68, Marriages 1736-54; vol. 2, Baptisms, Marriages and Burials 1719-35; vol. 3, Marriages 1754-80, Banns 1763-71; vol. 4, Marriages 1780-1813

see also Gloucestershire entry

Place Names

MAWER, A.M., STENTON, F.M., HOUGHTON, F.T.S., (eds.), *The English Place Name Society, vol. 4, Worcestershire* (1927)

Quarter Sessions

BUND, J.W., (ed.), 'Calendar of Worcester Quarter Sessions, 1591-1643'
   (*W.A.S.*, vol. 11, 1899-1900)
JOHNSON, H.C., and WILLIAMS, N.J., (eds.), *Quarter Session Records of
   Worcestershire* (1964)

School Registers

The Old Bromsgrovian Register, 1553-1643 (published by the *Bromsgrove Messenger*
   Company, 1908-10)

Subsidies

BUND, J.W.W., (ed.), 'Subsidy of 1280 in Worcestershire' (*W.A.S.*, vol. 1, 1893)
'Subsidy of 1327/8 in Worcestershire' (*W.A.S.*, vol. 4, 1895)
AMPHLETT, J., (ed.), 'Subsidy of 1332/3 in Worcestershire' (*W.A.S.*, vol. 10,
   1899)
AMPHLETT, J., (ed.), 'Subsidy of 1346/58 in Worcestershire' (*W.A.S.*, vol. 12,
   1900)
AMPHLETT, J., (ed.), 'Subsidies of 1427/9 and 1603 in Worcestershire'
   (*W.A.S.*, vol. 13, 1901)

Visitations

PHILLIMORE, W.P.W., (ed.), 'Visitation of Worcestershire, 1569' (*Harleian
   Society*, vol. 27, 1888)
BUTLER, A.T., (ed.), 'Visitation of Worcestershire, 1634' (*Harleian Society*, vol.
   90, 1938)
METCALFE, W.C., (ed.), *The Visitation of the County of Worcester, 1682-3* (1883)

Wills and Administrations

FRY, E.A., (ed.), 'Worcester Wills, 1451-1600' (*B.R.S.I.L.*, vol. 31, 1904)
FRY, E.A., (ed.), 'Worcester Wills, 1601-1652' (*B.R.S.I.L.*, vol. 39, 1910)

Yorkshire

Record Repositories and Libraries

Humberside County Record Office, County Hall, Beverley HU17 9BA
South Humberside Area Record Office, Town Hall Square, Grimsby

Kingston upon Hull City Record Office, 79 Lowgate, Kingston upon Hull
Leeds District Archives (West Yorkshire Archives Service), Chapeltown Road,
   Sheepscar, Leeds
Yorkshire Archaeological Society, Claremont, Clarendon Road, Leeds
Bradford Central Library (Archives Department), Prince's Way, Bradford
Calderdale Metropolitan Borough Archives Department, Central Library,
   Lister Lane, Halifax
Kirklees Library and Museums Service, Princess Alexandra Walk, Hudders-
   field
West Yorkshire Record Office (and Registry of Deeds), Newstead Road,
   Wakefield
Wakefield Metropolitan District Archives Department, Library Headquarters,
   Balne Lane, Wakefield
North Yorkshire County Record Office, County Hall, Northallerton, North
   Yorkshire DL7 8SG
North Yorkshire Record Office, The York Archives, Exhibition Square, York
The Borthwick Institute of Historical Research, University of York, St
   Anthony's Hall, Peasholme Green, York YO1 2PW
WEBB, C.C., *A Guide to the Genealogical Sources in the Borthwick Institute of Historical
   Research* (1981)
South Yorkshire Record Office, Cultural Activities Centre, Ellin Street,
   Sheffield S1 4PL
Sheffield City Libraries, Archives Division, Central Library, Surrey Street,
   Sheffield S1 1XZ
Doncaster Archives Department, King Edward Road, Balby, Doncaster
Brian O'Malley Library, Rotherham
A Brief Guide to Yorkshire Record Offices (1968)

Census

1851 Census Index, Holme on Spalding Moor, Bubwith, Aughton (*East Yorkshire
   Family History Society*)

Deeds

BROWN, W., et al (eds.), *Yorkshire Deeds* (*Yorkshire Archaeological Society Record
   Series*, vols. 39, 50, 63, 65, 69, 76, 83, 102, 111, 120, 1909-55)

Directories

WHITE, W., *Gazetteer of Leeds, Bradford, Halifax, Huddersfield, Wakefield and the whole
   of the Clothing Districts of the West Riding of Yorkshire* (1978 reprint of 1853 edn.)

Episcopal Registers and Records of Clergy

York registers are extant from 1225, except for 1255-66
The *Surtees Society* has published the following registers:
   Walter Gray, 1225-55 (vol. 56, 1892)

Walter Giffard, 1266-79 (vol. 109, 1904)
Walter Wickwane, 1279-85 (vol. 114, 1907)
John de Romeyn, 1286-96 (vols. 123 and 128, 1913, 1917)
Henry de Newark, 1296-9 (vol. 128, 1917)
Thomas of Corbridge, 1299-1303 (vols. 138 and 141, 1925, 1928)
William Greenfield, 1306-15 (vols. 145 and 149, 1931, 1934)
SMITH, D.M., (ed.), *A Calendar of the Register of Robert Waldby, Archbishop of York 1397* (1974)
SWANSON, R.N., (ed.), *A Calendar of the Register of Richard Scrope, Archbishop of York 1398-1405* (vol. 1, 1981)
LAWTON, G., *Collections relative to the Dioceses of York and Ripon* (2nd ed., 1842)
MCCALL, H.B., *Richmondshire Churches, with Lists of Incumbents* (1901)
THOMPSON, A.H., 'Registers of the Archdeaconry of Richmond, 1361-1477, with introduction and notes' (*Journal of the Yorkshire Archaeological Society*, vols. 15, 30, 32, 1896-1912)
'The Registers of the Archbishops of York' (*J.Y.A.S.*, vol. 32, 1912)
OLLARD, S.L., (ed.), 'Archbishop Herring's Visitation Returns, 1743' (*Y.A.S.R.S.*, vols. 71, 72, 75, 77, 79, 1928-31)
'East Riding Clergy, 1525-6' (*J.Y.A.S.*, vol. 25, 1916)
SHIELS, W.J., *Archbishop Grindal's Visitation of the Diocese of York 1575* (1977)
HORN, J.M., and SMITH, D.M., (eds.), *Fasti Ecclesiae Anglicanae: diocese of York 1541-1857* (1975)
LONGLEY, K.M., (ed.), *Ecclesiastical Cause Papers at York: the Dean and Chapter's Court, 1350-1843* (1980)

Family Histories

ENGLISH, B.A., *The Lords of Holderness 1086-1260* (1980)
GORDON, C., *By Gaslight in Winter: a Victorian Family through the Magic Lantern* (1980)
FREEMAN, C.B., *Mary Simpson of Boynton Vicarage* (1972)
HICKS, J.D., (ed.), *A Victorian Boyhood on the Wolds: the recollections of J.R. Mortimer* (1980)
BEASTALL, T.W., *A North Country Estate: the Saundersons and Lumleys* (1975)
MALLORY-SMITH, SHEILA, *A History of the Mallory Family* (1984)

Feet of Fines

'Yorkshire Feet of Fines, 1191-9' (*J.Y.A.S.*, vol. 11)
BROWN, W., (ed.), 'Yorkshire Feet of Fines, 1199-1214' (*Surtees Society*, vol. 94, 1897)
PARKER, J., (ed.), 'Yorkshire Feet of Fines, 1218-72' (*J.Y.A.S.*, vols. 62, 67, 82, 1921-32)
BAILDON, W.P., (ed.), 'Yorkshire Feet of Fines, 1327-77' (*J.Y.A.S.*, vols. 42, 52, 1910, 1915)
COLLINS, F., (ed.), 'Yorkshire Feet of Fines, 1486-1603' (*J.Y.A.S.*, vols. 2, 5, 7, 8, 1887-90)

BRIGG, W., (ed.), 'Yorkshire Feet of Fines, 1603-25' (*J.Y.A.S.*, vols. 53, 58, 1915, 1917)

Freemen

COLLINS, F., (ed.), 'Register of the Freemen of York, 1272-1759' (*S.S.*, vols. 96, 102, 1897, 1900)

Heraldry

BLOOM, J.H., *Heraldry in the Churches of the West Riding of Yorkshire* (6 vols., 1892-5)
SUMMERS, PETER (ed.), *Hatchments in Britain: vol. 3, the Northern Counties* (1979)
TURNER, J.H., *Coats of Arms of the Nobility and Gentry of Yorkshire* (1911)

Inquisitiones Post Mortem

BROWN, W., (ed.), 'Yorkshire Inquisitiones Post Mortem 1241-1307' (*J.Y.A.S.*, vols. 12, 23, 31, 36, 37, 1892-1906)
BAILDON, W.P., (ed.), 'Yorkshire Inquisitiones Post Mortem 1399-1422' (*J.Y.A.S.*, vol. 59, 1918)
'Yorkshire Inquisitiones Post Mortem, 1603-49' (*J.Y.A.S.*, vol. 1, 1885)

Manorial Records

HALL, T.W., *A Descriptive Catalogue of Manorial Records of Sheffield, Hallamshire* (1926-34)

Marriage Licences

'Paver's York Marriage Licences, 1567-1630' (*J.Y.A.S.*, vols. 7, 9, 11, 16, 17, 20)
'Consolidated Index to Paver's Marriage Licences, 1567-1630' (*Yorkshire Archaeological Society Extra Series*, vol. 2, 1912)
The *East Riding Family History Society* has published the following volumes:
Holmpton Marriages 1739-1837
Routh Marriages 1750-1837
Skipsea Marriages 1750-1837
Welwick Marriages 1739-1837
Sculcoates All Saints: Index to Marriages 1813-April 1817

Members of Parliament

'Members of Parliament for Aldborough and Boroughbridge, 1553-1700' (*J.Y.A.S.*, vol. 27)

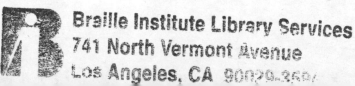

GOODER, A., (ed.), 'Parliamentary Representation of the County of Yorks., 1258-1832' (*Y.A.S.R.S.*, vols. 91, 96, 1935, 1938)

Monumental Inscriptions

The *East Riding Family History Society* has published the following volumes:
Easington Monumental Inscriptions
Lockington Monumental Inscriptions
Lund Monumental Inscriptions
Middleton on the Wolds Monumental Inscriptions
North Frodingham Monumental Inscriptions
Skerne Monumental Inscriptions
Lowthorpe Monumental Inscriptions

Muster Rolls

BAILDON, W.P., (ed.), 'Skyrack Wapentake, 1539' (*Thoresby Society*, vol. 4, 1895; vol. 9, 1899)
BAILDON, W.P., 'Claro Wapentake, 1535' (*T.S.*, vol. 15, 1909)

Parochial and Non-Parochial Registers

BARLEY, M.W., (ed.), 'Parochial Documents of the Archdeaconry of the East Riding' (*Y.A.S.R.S.*, vol. 99, 1939)
HUDSON, A.V., and WALKER, J.W., 'Index to Parish Register Transcripts in the Diocesan Registry, York' (*Y.A.S.R.S.*, vol. 74, 1929)
MORTIMER, J., and MORTIMER, R., *Leeds Friends Minute Book, 1692-1712* (1880)
'Non-Parochial Registers in Yorkshire' (*Bradford Antiquary*, n.s. vol. 1)
Publications of the *Yorkshire Parish Register Society*, 1899 onwards
GURNEY, N.K.M., *A Handlist of Parish Register Transcripts in the Borthwick Institute of Historical Research* (1976)

Pedigrees

CLAY, SIR CHARLES (ed.), 'Early Yorkshire Families' (*Yorkshire Archaeological Society Record Series* vol. 135, 1973)
FOSTER, J., *Pedigrees of the County Families of Yorkshire* (2 vols., 1874)
WALKER, J.W., (ed.), 'Yorkshire Pedigrees' (*Harleian Society*, vols. 94-6, 1942-4)

Place Names

SMITH, A.H., (ed.), *The English Place Name Society*, vols. 30, 31, 32, 33, 34, 35, 36, 37, *the West Riding* (1961, 1963)

SMITH, A.H., (ed.), *The English Place Name Society, vol. 14, the East Riding and York* (1937)
SMITH, A.H. (ed.), *The English Place Name Society, vol. 5, the North Riding* (1928)
Yorkshire Place Names

Quarter Sessions

LISTER, J., (ed.), 'West Riding Sessions Rolls, 1597/8-1642' (*Y.A.S.R.S.*, vols. 3, 54, 1888, 1915)
ATKINSON, J.C., (ed.), 'North Riding Sessions Rolls, 1605-1786' (*North Riding Record Society*, vols. 1-8, 1884-92)

School Registers

ATKINSON, H.B., (ed.), *Giggleswick School Register, 1499-1921* (1922)
WILSON, B., (ed.), *Sedbergh School Register, 1546-1895* (1909)

Subsidies

BROWN, W., (ed.), 'The Subsidy of 1297' (*Y.A.S.R.S.*, vol. 16, 1894)
BROWN, W., (ed.), 'The Subsidy of 1301' (*Y.A.S.R.S.*, vol. 21, 1897)
PARKER, J., (ed.), 'The Subsidy of 1327: North Riding and City of York' (*Y.A.S.R.S.*, vol. 74, 1929)
'Clerical Subsidies in the Province of York, 1632-4' (*J.Y.A.S.*, vol. 31)

Surnames

REDMONDS, G. (ed.), *English Surnames Series: vol. 1, Yorkshire, The West Riding* (1973)

Transportations

An alphabetical index to the men and women transported to America and Australia from the Beverley, East Riding, Hedon and Hull Quarter Sessions (*East Yorkshire Family History Society*, 1984)

Visitations

LONGSTAFFE, W.H.D., (ed.), 'Visitation of Yorkshire, 1530' (*S.S.*, vol. 41, 1863)
NORCLIFFE, C.B., (ed.), 'Visitation of Yorkshire, 1563-4' (*Harleian Society*, vol. 16, 1881)

FOSTER, J., (ed.), *Visitations of Yorkshire, 1584/5, 1612* (1875)
DAVIES, R., (ed.), 'Visitation of Yorkshire, 1665-6' (*S.S.*, vol. 36, 1859)
CLAY, J.W., (ed.), 'Visitation of Yorkshire, 1665-6' (*The Genealogist*, n.s. vol. 9)
CLAY, J.W., (ed.), *Drydale's Visitation of Yorkshire, 1665-6* (3 vols., 1899-1917)

Wills and Administrations

'Index of Wills in the York Registry, 1389-1688' (*Y.A.S.R.S.*, vols. 6, 11, 14, 19, 22, 24, 4, 26, 32, 35, 49, 60, 89, 1888-1934)
'Wills proved in the Court of the Dean and Chapter, 1321-1636' (*Y.A.S.R.S.*, vol. 38, 1907)
CROSSLEY, E.W., (ed.), 'Wills proved in the Yorkshire Consistory Court, 1427-1658 and in the Court of the Dean of York, 1604-1722' (*Y.A.S.R.S.*, vol. 73, 1928)
COLLINS, F., (ed.), 'Knaresborough Wills, 1509-1660' (*S.S.*, vols. 104, 110, 1902, 1905)
'Richmond Wills, 1442-1579' (*S.S.*, vol. 26, 1853)
COLLINS, F., (ed.), 'Selby Wills 1635-1710' (*Y.A.S.R.S.*, vol. 47, 1912)
RAINE, J., 'Testamenta Eboracensis, 1300-1551' (*S.S.*, vols. 4, 30, 45, 53, 79, 106, 1836-1903)
CLAY, J.W., (ed.), 'North Country Wills, 1383-1605' (*S.S.*, vols. 116, 121, 1908, 1912)
LUMB, G.D., (ed.), 'Testamenta Leodiensia, 1539-61' (*Thoresby Society*, vols. 19, 27, 1913, 1930)
'Wills proved in Wakefield Peculiar Court, 1587-1855' (*Northern Genealogist*, vols. 1 and 2)
PRESTON, W.E., 'Wills proved in the Manor of Crossley, Bingley, Cottingley, and Pudsey, with Inventories and Abstracts of Bonds 1559-1645' (*Bradford Historical and Antiquarian Society Local Record Series*, vol. 1, 1929)
CROSSLEY, E.W., 'Testamentary Documents of Yorkshire Peculiars' (*Y.A.S.R.S.*, vol. 74, 1929)
CHARLESWORTH, J., (ed.), 'Wills and Administrations in the Registers of Archbishops at York, 1316-1822' (*Y.A.S.R.S.*, vol. 93, 1937)

Ireland

Record Repositories and Libraries

General Register Office, Oxford House, 49-55 Chichester Street, Belfast BT1 4HL
Public Record Office of Northern Ireland, 66 Balmoral Avenue, Belfast BT9 6NY
General Register Office, Custom House, Dublin 1, Eire
The Genealogical Office, Dublin Castle, Dublin 2, Eire

The Public Record Office, Four Courts, Dublin 7, Eire (also houses the Probate Office)

The National Library of Ireland, Kildare Street, Dublin 2, Eire (Reader's ticket needed)

FALLEY, M.D., *Irish and Scotch-Irish Ancestral Research* (2 vols., 1981 reprint of 1962 edn.)

SMITH, F., and GARDNER, D.E., (eds.), *Genealogical Atlas of Ireland* (1972)

Directories

LOCKER, R., (ed.), *A Biographical Dictionary of Architects in Ireland* (1981)

WALLACE, M., *One Thousand Irish Lives* (1983)

Emigration Records

SCHLEGEL, D.M., *Passengers from Ireland 1811-17* (1980 reprint)

HACKETT, D.J., and EASLY, C.M., *Passenger Lists from Ireland 1811, 1815-16* (1981 reprint of 1931 edn.)

EILISH, E., *Emigrants from Ireland 1847-52* (1978 reprint of 1960 edn.)

DICKSON, R.J., *Ulster Emigration to Colonial America 1718-1775* (1976 reprint of 1966 edn.)

ADAMS, W.F., *Ireland and Irish Emigration to the New World from 1815 to the Famine* (1980 reprint of 1932 edn.)

Family Histories

MCKINNEY, W.F., *Sentry Hill: an Ulster Farm and Family 1832-1917* (1981)

ESTORICK, M., *Heirs and Graces: the claim to the Dukedom of Leinster* (1981)

ANTRIM, A., *The Antrim McDonnels* (1979)

WEIR, H.W.L., *O'Brien People and Places* (1983)

Heraldry

GALLOWAY, PETER, *The Most Illustrious Order of St Patrick* (1983)
Marriage Licences

ffOLIOT, ROSEMARY, *Index to Raphoe Marriage Licence Bonds 1710-55 and 1817-30*

Monumental Inscriptions

The *Ulster Historical Foundation* has published some 20 volumes under the editorship of R.J.S. Clarke.

Parochial and Non-Parochial Registers

BARR, N.C., and KERR, W.C., (eds.), *The Oldest Register of the Parish of Derriaghy, County Antrim* (1981)

Pedigrees

MONTGOMERY-MASSINGBERD, H., (ed.), *Burke's Irish Family Records* (5th revised edition, 1976)
O'HART, J., *Irish Pedigrees: the Origin and Stem of the Irish Nation* (1976 reprint of 5th revised edition)
O'HART, J., *Irish and Anglo-Irish Landed Gentry* (1968 reprint of 1884 edn.)
MACLYSAGHT, E., *Irish Families: their Names, Origin and Arms* (1972)

Place Names

O'CONNELL, J., *The Meaning of Irish Place Names* (1980)

Surnames

BREFFNY, BRIAN DE, *Irish Family Names: arms, origin and location* (1982)
MACLYSAGHT, E., *The Surnames of Ireland* (1978)
MATHESON, SIR ROBERT, *The Special Report on the Surnames in Ireland and Varieties and Synonyms of Surnames and Christian Names in Ireland* (1968 reprint)

Visitations

HOWARD, J.J., and CRISP, F.J., *The Visitation of Ireland: pedigrees and illustrations of arms* (reprint of 1897 and 1918 edns.)

Scotland

Record Repositories and Libraries

Scottish Record Office, PO Box 36, H.M. General Register House, Princes Street, Edinburgh EH1 3YT
National Library of Scotland, George IV Bridge, Edinburgh EH1 1EW
HAMILTON-EDWARDS, GERALD, *In Search of Scottish Ancestry* (1983 new edition)
STUART, M., *Scottish Family History* (1978 reprint of 11930 edn.)

SMITH, F., *Genealogical Atlas of Scotland*
SMITH, F., *Genealogical Gazetteer of Scotland* (1979 reprint)

Clan Histories

MONCRIEFFE, SIR IAIN OF THAT ILK, *The Highland Clans* (1981 edn.)
GRIMBLE, IAN, *Clans and Chiefs* (1980)
MACDONALD, D.J., *Clan Donald* (1979)
STRATHSPEY, LORD, *A History of Clan Grant* (1983)
MACLAREN, M., *The MacLarens* (1978)
SHAW, MAJOR C.J., *A History of Clan Shaw* (1983)
WALLIS, G.A., *Sagas of the Wallis Clan* (1978)
GRANT, I.F., *The MacLeods* (1981)

Emigration Records

CAMERON, V.R., *Emigrants from Scotland to America 1774-5* (1980 reprint of 1930 edn.)

Family Histories

ANDERSON, M., *Anderson Families* (1984)
LINDSAY AND COYSH, *Inverary and the Dukes of Argyll* (1974)
CAMERON, D.K., *Willie Gavin, Crofter Man* (1980)

Heraldry

URQUHART, R.M., *Scottish Burgh and County Heraldry* (1973)
URQUHART, R.M., *Scottish Civic Heraldry* (1979)

Parochial and Non-Parochial Records

STEEL, D. J. (ed.), *National Index of Parish Registers, vol. XII, Sources for Scottish Genealogy and Family History* (1981 reprint)

Place Names

JOHNSON, J.B., *Place Names of Scotland* (1970 reprint of 1934 edn.)

Surnames

LAMB, G., *Orkney Surnames* (1981)

Wills and Administrations

GRANT, Francis J. (ed.), 'Commisariot of Edinburgh: Testaments 1514-1600'
(*British Record Society Index Library*, vol. 16, 1897)
GRANT, Francis J. (ed.), 'Commisariot of Inverness:Testaments 1630-1800;
Commisariot of Hamilton and Camsie: Testaments 1564-1800' (*B.R.S.I.L.*,
vol. 20, 1898)

Wales

Record Repositories and Libraries

Gwent County Record Office, County Hall, Cwmbran, Gwent NP4 2XH
Gwynedd Archives Service, Anglesey Area Record Office, Shire Hall, Llangefni
LL77 7TW
Gwynedd Archives Service, Dolgellau Area Record Office, Cae Penarlag,
Dolgellau, Gwynedd
Gwynedd Archives Service, Caernafon Area Record Office, County Offices,
Shirehall Street, Caernafon
Glamorgan Archives Service, County Hall, Cathays Park, Cardiff CF1 3NE
Dyfed Archives, Pembrokeshire Record Office, The Castle, Haverfordwest,
Dyfed
Dyfed Archives Service, Carmarthenshire Record Office, County Hall, Carmar-
then SA31 1JP
National Library of Wales, Aberystwyth, Dyfed SY23 3BU
Dyfed Archives, Ceredigion Record Office, Aberystwyth, Dyfed
Clwyd Record Office, 46 Clwyd Street, Ruthin LL15 1HP
Clwyd Record Office, The Old Rectory, Hawarden, Deeside CH5 3NR
HAMILTON-EDWARDS, G., *In Search of Welsh Ancestry* (1985)

Ecclesiastical Registers and Records of Clergy

LE NEVE, J., (ed.), *Fasti Ecclesiae Anglicanae: the Welsh Dioceses 1300-1541* (1965)

GLOSSARY

Abjuration of the Realm: Promises made to go abroad for ever (later, to a special place in England) made by a suspected criminal who has taken sanctuary.

Abutment: the shorter sides of a piece of land are said to abut upon adjacent plots; abutments describe the boundaries.

Accountant: person rendering account.

Act Book: the day to day account of the Ordinary's legal proceldures. Usually the Act Books are divided separately, for probate acts relating to wills and administrations. All sorts of matters, including marriage licences, may be recorded in the bishop's Act Books, as well as sentences and permits to clergy, schoolmasters, surgeons, midwives, apothecaries, and watchmakers, with licences for tuition and guardianship.

Administrator: one who has entered into a bond before the court to administer the estate, the right to do which has been granted by the court.

Ad Quod Damnum: enquiries made to escheators of counties or districts when any grant for market, fair, etc., or licence for alienation of land was solicited, to ensure that such a grant was not prejudicial to the interests of the Crown.

Advowson: right of presentation to a benefice, i.e., a person could be nominated by a patron to a bishop for institution into a living of the church.

Affidavit: written statement, voluntarily made under oath.

Aid: written statement, voluntarily made under oath.

Alienation: transference of property from one person to another.

Allocate: undertaking by Exchequer accountants of all manner of royal business involving expenditure under units of computate.

Alnage: *see* ulnage.

Amercement: payment by offender 'in the mercy' of the court.

Amortisation: alienation in mortmain (*q.v.*).

Annates: profits of a benefice for the first year after a voidancy. Their payment to the Pope was instituted by John XXII and made perpetual by Boniface IX.

Answer: (a) statement of a criminal's case; (b) affidavit in reply to an interrogatory.

Appeal: (a) form of criminal accusation; (b) reference of a suit from a lower to a higher court.

Apposer: Exchequer official charged with 'apposal' or examination of sheriffs.

Approver: (a) felon allowed to 'appeal' (accuse) accomplices; (b) one who 'improved' or exploited an estate.

Archive: historical record.

Armiger: strictly, a person entitled to bear a coat of arms; used more generally in practice to mean a gentleman or an esquire.

Array: levy of men for armed service.

Arrentation: (a) commutation of service for rent; (b) imposition of rent (on assarts, etc.).

Assart: former woodland or waste brought under cultivation.

Assignment: (or assignation): (a) transference of a title to property, of a claim to repayment, etc.; (b) right given to some person or persons to administer an estate through the transference of that right from one person to another in the administration of the property.

Assize: (a) regulation (e.g., as to brewing or weaving); (b) procedure to establish possession of land, etc.; (c) itinerant court, originally designed for such procedures.

Associates: common law officials charged with keeping records, etc.

Attachment: (a) seizure of persons or goods, especially procedure to enforce finding of securities for appearance before a court or tribunal; (b) preliminary investigation of forest offences for which suspects had been attached.

Attainder, attaint: deprivation of rights (including those of heirs) consequent on conviction of treason or felony.

Attermination: fixing of terms for payment by instalments.

Attestation: formal confirmation by signature in the presence of witnesses.

Attorney: (a) person appointed to represent another; (b) professional representation in a court of common law.

Aula Regis: household court held in the 'King's Hall'.

Bail: surety (often in lieu of imprisonment) for appearance in court by an accused person or a party to a civil action.

Bail bond: surety for release of a ship, etc., pending judgement.

Bailiff: (a) a servant or agent for the management of an estate; (b) local official, usually subordinate to sheriff.

Ballastage: toll payable for the right to take in ballast.

Banneret: knight of superior rank.

Bargain and Sale: conveyance of estate, etc., for a valuable consideration.

Benefice: an ecclesiastical preferment held for life, especially a living with cure of souls held by a rector or vicar of a parish church.

Beneficiary: one who receives any benefit from the property.

Benevolence: a tax levied under the guise of a voluntary loan.

Bill, billa: (a) short, informal document; (b) a petition by a plaintiff initiating action in equity; (c) a brief written statement initiating proceedings at common law.

Bill of Middlesex: bill preliminary to the issue of a writ of *latitat* (*q.v.*).

Bill of Sale: deed witnessing assignment of property, especially with a view to settlement of debt or as a means of providing security.

Blanching: assay of sample coins by 'combustion' to test their silver content.

Bona Notabilia: simply means goods of note. It is taken to mean that the deceased person's estate has a value of at least £5.

Bond: an obligation entered into, usually in an ecclesiastical court, in respect of the granting of a licence or probate act. The document is signed, sealed and witnessed for the person promising to perform the provisions of the conditions detailed in the instrument.

Bordar: a serf of the lowest rank.

Breve: *see* writ.

Brief Book: register of printer's receipts for church briefs (i.e., licences for church collections in aid of specified charities).

Bull, bulla: leaden or other metallic seal, or letter, especially papal, sealed therewith.

Butlerage: duty of 2s. per tun on imported wine, levied by the king's butler.

Cadet: younger son or brother.

Calendar: (a) summary of contents of a series of documents, in the original language or translation; (b) list of prisoners brought to trial at a criminal court; (c) an index in consecutive sequence. Particularly applicable to lists of names of testators and intestate persons for whom probate has been granted.

Capias: writ ordering an arrest.

Capias in Manum: writ ordering seizure of goods or lands into the king's hand.

Cartulary: entry-book of charges.

Carucage: tax on ploughland: c.f. hidage.

Case stated: statement of questions of law or the facts and grounds of a determination or award for consideration by a higher court.

Catalogue: enumeration of documents or other objects (e.g., seals), of a particular form, or relating to a particular subject, irrespective of their provenance.

Causa Captionis, de: writ ordering certification as to cause of seizure of land etc., into king's hand.

Causes: civil proceedings at law or in equity, including actions and suits, as distinct from 'matters' (statutory proceedings in equity commenced by petition, motion, summons, etc.).

Caveat: a notice given by a person interested in a will warning the probate court not to take action without their case being heard.

Cestui que use: the one who has the use and profit of land, the title of which is vested in another.

Certiorari: writ or bill directing that a court be certified or informed on some matter, especially on the record of an action heard in an inferior court.

Chantry: endowment for the singing of masses for the souls of the dead.

Chapel, Free: chapel exempt from ecclesiastical jurisdiction.

Charge: *see* onus.

Charter: (a) original grants in perpetuity of privileges, lands, and other possessions to corporations and individuals, and also the creation of peerages; (b) charters of confirmation or *inspeximus* of previous grants, which were usually recited in full, and to which further privileges were sometimes added.

Chasm: otherwise referred to as a 'hiatus' or 'vacancy' – a loss of records or break in the sequence of records, often because the court concerned was closed.

Chirograph: deed, etc., written in duplicate or multiplicate, especially in form of indenture (q.v.).

Class (of records): The public records are arranged in groups according to the several courts or departments from which they emanated, e.g. Exchequer, Admiralty, and each group is divided into 'classes'. To each class is assigned a 'class name', e.g. Exchequer, King's Remembrancer: Accounts, Various, and a class number, e.g. E.101.

Close: a part of common land enclosed.

Coast Bonds: (a) bonds entered into by shippers engaged in the coast trade not to land goods except at the ports declared; (b) certificates by port officials of the fulfilment of the bonds; (c) orders by customs officials to allow goods to pass coastwise to be landed at a stated English port; (d) analogous documents.

Cocket: customs house seal, or document sealed therewith and serving as a receipt for customs duties.

Codicil: a signed and witnessed addition to a will after it has been made.

Cognovit: acknowledgement of debt, authorising summary recovery in default of specified performance.

Collection: a gathering together of related materials.

College: a corporation of clergy, etc.

Combustion: *see* blanching.

Commendam: commitment of benefices, etc., to someone other than the incumbent.

Commissary Court: a court commissioned to carry out the duties of a superior authority in a particular district by delegating power, particularly in the granting of probates and of letters of administration.

Commission: grant or appointment to special authority or office.

Commitment: entrusting or consigning, especially to custody, before a trial.

Committiture: certificate of commitment to custody of a marshal.

Common Law: traditional English law, administered in the king's courts as distinct from local customary law, statute and equity.

Computate: writ addressed to the Treasurers and Barons of the Exchequer ordering an allowance to be made to the Exchequer Accountants for expenditure incurred by them out of monies for which they were accountable.

Conge d'Elire: authority by the crown to a dean and chapter for the election of a bishop.

Consistory Court: a court of ecclesiastical causes, presided over by church officials or dignitaries.

Constat: certificate, by the Clerk of the Pipe or auditors, or a matter on record. C.f. *inspeximus*.

Contrariants: adherents of the Earl of Lancaster in opposition to Edward II.

Controller, Comptroller: originally keeper of a counter-roll as a check on a collector or another accountant.

Contumace Capiendo, de: writ ordering commitment to lay custody of a person pronounced 'contumacious' by an ecclesiastical court.

Conveyance: transference by deed or writing of property from one person to another.

Coparceners: tenants, usually sisters, inheriting jointly.

Copyhold: a tenancy of land under the lord of the manor, recorded on the official roll of the court baron, a copy of the appropriate entry having been handed to the tenant as his title deed.

Cornage: a form of rent fixed by the number of horned cattle owned.

Corpus Comitatus: sum of rents and profits accounted for by a sheriff.

Corpus cum causa: writ ordering production in court of a person committed to prison, especially for debt, together with a record of his case.

Corrody: allowance of food, etc., by a religious house, especially as granted to the crown or another benefactor for maintenance of a retired servant.

Cottar: peasant who occupies a farm cottage and works as an out-servant.

Coucher, cowcher: large cartulary or the like.

Court Baron: the court of honourable service; the customary court of the manor.

Court Roll: record of proceedings in a manorial court, citable as evidence of copyhold.

Credence, letters of: written recommendation, especially of diplomatic credentials.

Curation: guardianship of orphaned minors.

Cursitor or Clerk of Course: an official of the Court of Chancery who made out all original writs and processes returnable in the court of King's Bench and elsewhere.

Curtesy, courtesy: the fee tail of a wife's property after her death or the life interest of her husband in her fee simple.

Curtilage: land or ground close to the dwelling house, usually enclosed.

Custodia Commissa, de: writ committing custody of lands, etc., or of a minor, etc., to a specified keeper or guardian.

Debenture: certificate of indebtedness, especially by the crown, surviving, after cancellation, as a receipt.

Declaration: (a) part of a judgement expressing a court's decision on a question of law; (b) first pleading delivered by the plaintiff; (c) summary procedure for auditing accounts.

Decree: judgement in a court of equity, either 'final' or 'interlocutory' (reserving the possibility of further consideration); distinct from 'order', which might be merely procedural.

Dedimus Bill: abstract of a bill in a Chancery suit on which commissioners were empowered by *dedimus potestatem* to take depositions.

Dedimus potestatem: writ or commission giving authority to perform certain official acts.

Deed Poll: deed made by one person or by persons having the same interest; distinct from an indenture, which involved two or more parties.

Deforciant: defendant in (fictitious) suit settled by fine; final agreement.

Demesne: land held by feudal or manorial lord for his own use.

Demesne, ancient: land held in demesne by the crown in the time of Edward the Confessor, as recorded in Domesday Book.

Demise: grant of estate, usually for limited term.

Demurrer: objection on a point of law to claim made by opposite party.

Denization: limited naturalisation of aliens; before 1844 they could be fully naturalised only by an act of Parliament.

Deposition: statement on oath, especially a written statement admissible in lieu of production of a witness.

Devise: gift or deposition, especially by will.

Diem Clausit Extremum: writ ordering inquiry as to lands held by a tenant-in-chief, on information that he has 'closed his last day'.

Disentailment: removal of entail restricting power to dispose of estate.

Dismission: decree whereby a Chancery bill is dismissed out of court.

Dispensation: exemption from an obligation of ecclesiastical law.

Disseisin: dispossession of land, etc., of seisin.

Disseisin, Novel: recent dispossessions, as ground for possessory assize.

Distraint, distress: seizure of chattels in order to enforce payment of debt, appearance in court, etc.; might be ordered by writ of *distringas* and revoked by *districtionem relaxes*.

Docket, docquet: (a) note or abstract of judgement; (b) abstract of warrant for grant; (c) note on official paper of action taken; (d) index slip forming means of reference to a registered file.

Dorse: the reverse side of a document or back of a page; hence *endorsement*, when information is added on the back.

Double Probate: when one of the named executors of a will was unable to act or to be present at the time of the granting of the probate, a subsequent grant of probate to the remaining executors is sometimes designated as a double probate.

Dower: the third part of the lands and tenements of a deceased husband, held as the life interest of a wife.

Droits: rights or perquisites, especially those attached to office of the Lord High Admiral or enjoyed by the crown in time of war.

Easement: a right of way over adjoining property; any privilege without profit.

Ejectment: action for recovery of possession, or later of title.

Elegit: writ ordering the seizure of a debtor's goods and half his land, when a creditor 'has chosen' this method of execution.

Enclosure Award: approved scheme for allotment of open fields and common waste of a manor.

Englishry: proof that man on whom an inquest was held was English (not Norman, etc.) in order to avoid a fine for murder.

Enrolment: entry on a roll or later in a book.

Entail: the division or settlement of an estate without regard to the usual rules or customs for its descent.

Entry: (a) note written in a book or roll, especially as a memorandum or a precedent; (b) going into a piece of land, actually or notionally, with the intention of asserting a right therein.

Equity: system of rules administered by Chancery, etc., supplementary to common law.

Escheat: reversion of a tenement to its feudal lord or to the crown, for default of an heir, or for treason or felony.

Escheator: official concerned with crown revenues derived from escheat, wardship of minors and other feudal incidents.

Essoin: excuse for non-appearance in court.

Estreat: extract from, or copy of, a record, especially of amercements, etc., creating crown debts to be levied by the Exchequer.

Exaction, exigent: repeated summons of a defendant in a county court, sometimes by writ of *exigi facias*, leading, in cases of default, to outlawry.

Exception: objection in pleading, especially on grounds of insufficiency.

Excise: duty imposed on the manufacture and sale of spirits etc., within the country.

Excommunication: exclusion from communion of the church, especially as a means of enforcing an ecclesiastical judgement.

Exemplification: sealed official copy of a document.

Exhibit: document, etc., produced in court and referred to in evidence.

Exigent, exigi facias: *see* exaction.

Extent: valuation of goods or lands.

Eyre(iter): circuit of justices.

Faculty: licence by an ecclesiastical superior to hold an office or to perform an act otherwise forbidden.

Fee: (a) the fief or reward or payment for service. Estate may be held in consideration of such service, upon condition of performance of feudal service, payment of dues or military provision; (b) hereditary tenement held by feudal service; (c) payment due to an official.

Fee-Farm Rent: perpetual rent imposed on a grantee of land in fee, especially as composition for a farm previously paid.

Fee Simple: absolute and unqualified inheritance of estate either by knight service or socage.

Fee Tail: limited inheritance of an estate.

Feet of Fines: record of transfer of land.

Felony: criminal offence entailing forfeiture of land and goods as well as death penalty.

Feodary: official concerned with the exercise of feudal rights.

Feoffee to Uses: the person holding common law estate so that another may enjoy its use or profit.

Ferriage: ferry, toll.

Feudal Incidents: obligations incident to feudal service, such as the payment of aids and reliefs, wardship of an heir during his minority, etc.

Feudal tenure: feudal tenure of land, subject to feudal service (originally military) and incidents and assured by fealty and homage.

Fiat: (a) authorisation, especially by the Attorney General, or by the Chancellor (e.g. of a bankruptcy procedure); (b) note of the making of such an authorisation.

Fieri Facias: writ ordering the levy of a specified sum from a debtor's goods in payment of a debt.

Filazer: official concerned with the filing of writs, etc.

File: set of separate documents purposely kept together, originally by a string or gut threaded through them.

Fine: (a) payment to the crown, especially by an offender; (b) payment to a feudal lord, especially for alienation of a tenement; (c) final concord used as a mode of conveyance.

First Fruits: profits of a benefice for the first year after a voidancy.

Folk-Moot: general assembly of people of a town, city or shire.

Forest: land held or granted by crown subject to special laws for preservation of game.

Forfeiture: loss of land or goods falling to crown or (in earlier usage) to feudal lord in consequence of misdeed.

Franchise: right to vote: *see* liberty.

Frank/Free Tenure: free holding of land.

Frankpledge, view of: list of persons standing on good behaviour: members of tithing mutually responsible for the good conduct or damage done by any one of the others.

Freehold: the tenancy of real estate of land held by right of inheritance, by purchase or by gift providing absolute ownership under the crown subject only to the fee simple of allegiance. In earlier times, a freehold tenant was distinguished as one who paid a purely nominal rent for the tenancy of land of the lord, their tenure being regarded as free and not servile.

Fugitive: one who has fled to escape trial for felony.

Gaol delivery: trail of prisoners detailed on criminal charges.

Gemot: moot, national assembly or council.

Gentleman: a well-born, well-mannered man, usually entitled to bear a coat of arms.

Green Wax: summonses for new debts sent to sheriff in respect of his shire.

Group: collective term for the records emanating from a particular court or department.

Guild: association of craftsmen, traders, etc., for socio-religious or professional purposes.

Habeas Corpus: writ ordering production in court of a person held in custody.

Halmote: hall-moot, manorial court.

Hanaper: financial department of the Chancery.

Havener: overseer of a haven.

Heriot: dues to the lord upon the death of a customary tenant in a manor; may also be due from free holders in the form of the tenant's best beast or a money composition.

Heptarchy: the seven kingdoms of the Angles and Saxons.

Hereditament: property that can be inherited; tangible (corporeal) and intangible (incorporeal) rights and property from land and funds held in trust.

Hidage: a land tax, assessed according to the number of 'hides', i.e., units of variable acreage, sometimes equated with 'carucates' or 'ploughlands' of (?)100-120 acres. *See* carucage.

Hobler: lightly-armed horseman.

Homage: ceremonial acknowledgement by free feudal tenant in return for his land that he is his lord's 'man'.

Honour: a seigneury of several manors held by or under one lord.

Honour Court: the court having jurisdiction over the group of manors and incidents of the lord of an honour; c.f. court baron, the court having jurisdiction over a manor.

Hundred: district forming part of a county.

Imparlance: allowance of time for pleading, ostensibly to permit discussion between parties with a view to settlement.

Imprest, prest: (a) payment in advance; (b) credit given before account.

Incident: the rights and records of rights, often for profit such as wardship and maritagium, heriot and surrender enjoyed by the lord of a manor.

Incidents: *see* feudal incidents.

Incumbent: holder of an ecclesiastical benefice.

Incumbered estate: estate burdened with mortgage or other liability.

Indenture: deed (chirograph) between two or more parties, originally divided along an indented line as a safeguard against forgery.

Index: alphabetical guide to persons or places named in documents.

Indictment: formal accusation of crime, especially one preferrred to and presented by a grand jury.

Indulgence: remission (after absolution) of punishment due to sin.

Inhibition: (a) a writ forbidding a dignitary or official of a court from proceeding further in a cause before him; (b) the closure of a court during the visition of a superior official, a judge, archbishop, bishop, etc. A court may also be inhibited by custom for months, years or on special occasions, during which time the business might be conducted by a higher court. (c) a writ, especially to an inferior ecclesiastical court, forbidding further proceedings in a case, or during a period of jurisdiction of another authority.

Innovate: writ directing the renewal of a lost tally.

Inquisition, inquest: inquiry by means of sworn testimony, sometimes instituted by a writ of *inquiras*.

Inquisitiones Post Mortem: enquiries made on a person's death to ascertain what payments, etc., were due to the king, and to grant the inheritance to the rightful heir.

Inspeximus: exemplification of a record (distinct from *innotescimus* or *vidimus*, copy of a document not of record); c.f. *constat*.

Inspeximus Charters: charters in which the grantor vouches to have inspected an earlier charter which he recites and confirms. They may be fictitious.

Instance: judicial cognisance, especially of contracts or injuries on the high seas.

Institution: commitment of cure of souls to an incumbent by a bishop or his representative.

Instruction Books: apparently fee books of the Clerk of Indictments, containing particulars of presentments drawn up by him for a grand jury.

Instrument: a formal legal writing (civil law).

Interlocutory: incidental or provisional (not definitive) decree.

Interrogatory: written questions put to witnesses out of court, answerable by deposition.

Intrusion: unlawful entry into possession of vacant lands, etc.

Inventory: a list of personal and household effects, goods and chattels with their value, appraised by the auditors or officers commissioned to carry out the survey at the time of the owner's death.

Issue: (a) matter of fact or law, affirmed by one and denied by another party to an action at common law and made into a decisive question between them; (b) money paid out or derived from specific source.

Jury: sworn body of men (jurors), originally summoned to testify to facts, later required to decide on issue submitted.

Knight's service: military service which a knight was bound to do as a condition for holding his lands.

Latitat: King's Bench writ summoning a defendant deemed to be resident in Middlesex (and thus within the jurisdiction of the court) but 'lurking' elsewhere.

Lease and Release: conveyance of fee simple of land by lease for a year, followed immediately by release (q.v.) of reversion.

Leasehold: property held by a lease or rental contract for a given period.

Leet: (a) a meeting of the ways; (b) the district of the court; (c) court held to take the view of frankpledge and fealty.

Letters Missive: letter conveying command, recommendation or permission, especially *conge d'elire*.

Letters of Administration: the grant to a named person, often the next of kin, who has applied to the probate court for permission to administer the property and distribution of the effects of a person who has not left a valid will.

Letters Patent: *see* patent.

Levari Facias: writ ordering levy of a specified sum from lands, etc.

Libel: (a) defamation in a permanent form; (b) first written plea or complaint (civil or canon law).

Liberate: (a) rolls containing emoluments of units under the Great Seal relating to expenditure: (b) writs addressed to the Treasurer and Chamberlains of the Exchequer and ordering payments to be made out of the Treasury.

Liberty, franchise: (a) royal privilege enjoyed locally by a subject, by grant or prescription; (b) area within which such is enjoyed.

List: (a) numerical: enumerating items comprising a particular class of records, usually indicating little more than the dates covered by each item; (b) descriptive: in which the items are more fully described.

Livery: (a) delivery, handing over, of seisin, etc; (b) allowance to a servant, etc. for maintenance, especially in the form of special dress.

Mainprise: appointment of sureties or mainpenors for the appearance of a prisoner, etc.

Mandamus: (a) writ ordering performance of an official duty; (b) writ issued a year after the death of a tenant-in-chief, directing an escheator to hold an inquisition.

Manor: a territorial domain which may be held by a person directly from the crown or as the sub-tenant of the lord of an honour or of a larger manor. The manor was a territory often encompassing more than one parish or parts of parishes, over which the lord had jurisdiction in respect of the use of that territory and the good behaviour and fealty of those living within its bounds. The jurisdiction would be carried out by the customary usages of the manorial courts, the court-leet in respect of law and order and the court baron in respect of the use of land and manorial property. Some manors had the right to give probate for wills.

Manor court rolls: records of the proceedings of a manorial court.

Maritagium: the right of a lord to dispose of an infant heir of one of his tenants in marriage. The husband of a female heiress would be expected to perform her feudal obligations.

Marque, Letters of: commission to a captain or the owner of a private ship authorising warlike action against enemy ships.

Marshalsea: (a) office of marshal (entrusted with prisoners, etc.); (b) prison for which a marshal was responsible.

Master: Chancery official.

Matters: *see* causes.

Membrane: *see* roll.

Memoranda: *see* remembrancer.

Mesne: intermediate, with reference to a legal process or to feudal tenure.

Messuage: a house or dwelling, usually including the outbuildings.

Minister: general term for a servant, agent or official.

Minor: a person under legal age, formerly 21 years.

Misae: expenses, outlay.

Misdemeanour: common law offence not amounting to felony.

Mittimus: writ transmitting record, usually in response to *certiorari*.

Moiety: the half or division of property.

Monitions: summonses, usually from a superior to a lower court to release certain documents required in a case before it.

Mortmain, Alienation in: grant of land, etc., to a religious house or other corporation, in effect depriving the crown or another feudal lord of incidents due on death of a tenant.

Motion: application to a court or judge.

Muniment: title deeds; evidence of rights and privileges.

Naturalisation: *see* denization.

Nichil: late Latin spelling of *nihil*, 'nothing'.

Nisi Prius: trial by jury at the London and Middlesex sessions or at the assizes; originally ordered to be held at a central court 'unless previously' held before justices on circuit.

Non Omittas: writ ordering sheriff not to omit execution of a writ by reason of a liberty.

Non sunt inventi: notification that a specified person or persons 'have not been found'.

Nonae: subsidy of a ninth of the corn, wool and lambs in each parish.

Nuncupative wills: oral testaments written down by witnesses who swear to the truth of the statements. Such wills were dictated by the testator in poor health or on his deathbed.

Oblata Nova: new oblations (offerings or payments) to the crown.

Obventions: customary offering or payment.

Odio et atia de: writ ordering an inquiry as to whether a charge of murder has been brought through 'hatred and malice'.

Onus: charge, sum total debited to an accountant, from which payments and allowances (discharge) were then deducted.

Order: *see* decree.

Ordnance: military stores, munitions.

Outlawry: putting 'outside the law' (making liable to capital sentence or imprisonment and forfeiture) as the ultimate means to compel an appearance in court or obedience to a court order.

Oyer and Terminer: commission to justices to 'hear and determine' specified treasons, felonies and misdemeanours, or all such committed within a specified district.

Palaeography: the study of ancient writing and inscriptions.

Palatinate: area in which an earl or bishop exercised adminstrative and juridical rights elsewhere reserved to the crown.

Patent, Letters Patent: sealed open letter embodying a grant by a private person or by the crown of estate, right, liberty, etc., especially (in modern usage) of monopoly of new invention.

Pawn: panel, parchment strip containing a list of names.

Peace, Commission of the: appointment of justices to hold sessions for the keeping of the king's peace within a specified county.

Peculiar: where one or more parishes are controlled for purposes of probate or grants of administration or other ecclesiastical causes by a different jurisdiction than the Ordinary's, this area is referred to as a peculiar.

Peculiar jurisdiction: exemption from the authority of a bishop as Ordinary (*judex ordinarius*) within his diocese.

Pell: parchment or 'skin' (*pellis*) containing a note of monies paid or received.

Perambulation: beating the bounds, delimitation.

Personal Action: action to enforce remedy against a person, as distinct from 'real' action (for recovery of a thing).

Personality: the goods, chattels, credits, and personal property as distinct from real land and property.

Pesour: Exchequer official charged with checking weight of coinage.

Petty Bag: department of Chancery, originally dealing with cases affecting the crown, of which the records were kept apart in *parva* bags.

Pipe, Pipe Rolls: name given to the Great Roll of the Exchequer, apparently because of its shape when rolled up.

Plea, *placitum*: action at law.

Pleadings: formal statements by parties to an action, sometimes excluding declaration.

Postea: (a) note of subsequent proceedings added to an entry on rolls, etc.; (b) record omitted from roll etc., and preserved separately.

Post-fine and pre-fine: fines payable to the king from a Writ of Government.

Posting: formal entry in an account book.

Practice book, attorney's: book of rules, precedents, etc., otherwise called 'protonotary's instructor'.

Precipe, praecipe: (a) instruction for issuing a writ; (b) writ ordering a sheriff to command a tenant to give up land.

Presentation: nomination by a patron to a bishop, etc., of a person to be instituted to a benefice.

Presentment: report by jury or peace officers, especially by a grand jury acting without a bill of indictment.

Primogeniture: principle, custom or law by which title or inheritance descends to the eldest son (or eldest child).

Prise, prisage: royal rights to take wine etc. for use of the household, later commuted to a payment; e.g. butlerage.

Privateer: ship commissioned by letters of marque to exercise general reprisals.

Privilege: grant to an individual, corporation or class of a right or immunity not generally enjoyed by them.

Prize: ship, etc., captured at sea in virtue of rights of war.

Probate: when a document offered as the last will and testament of a deceased person has been accepted by the court, it is said to have been proved and when the executors, trustees or other persons made responsible for its execution have submitted the evidence and been granted permission to carry out the provisions of the will, probate is effected.

Process: (a) entire course of procedure in a legal action; (b) summons to appear in court.

Proclamation: public notice on any subject, issued by authority.

Proctor, procurator: civil and canon law equivalent of an attorney.

Proffer: provisional payment by a sheriff before an audit.

Proof of age: testimony (to some extent fictitous) that the heir to a feudal tenement is of age to receive seisin.

Protection: exemption, especially of one going overseas on the king's service, from certain legal proceedings and other liabilities.

Prothonotary, protonotary: title borne by the chief clerk in various courts.

Provenance: source of a document, especially the court or department in which it originated or was originally preserved.

Purgation: clearance from accusation, especially by the oath of the accused person supported by their neighbours.

Purpresture: encroachment, especially on the royal demesne or highway.

Purveyance: supply or exaction of provisions, especially for the royal household.

Pye: alphabetical index.

Pyx: box containing samples of coins issued each year from the Mint, submitted to ceremonial trial by weights and assay.

Quare Maneria, etc.: writ directing a tenant of manors, etc., to show why they should not be seized into the king's hand.

Quarter Sessions: statutory quarterly sessions of Justices of the Peace.

Quietus: auditor's note at the foot of an account, signifying that the account is 'quit', (i.e., discharged free of debt).

Quo ad bona: this term is found in the Lichfield probate calendars, indicating that the deceased person resided outside the jurisdiction of the court.

Quo titulo clamat: writ directing the tenant of an estate, etc., to show 'by what title he claims'.

Quo Warranto: procedure grounded on writ directing a claimant to a liberty (q.v.) etc., to show 'by what warrant' he claims.

Quominus: a writ by which almost anyone can institute in the Exchequer proceedings in any personal action and in ejectment.

Rack-rental: highest rent that a tenement will fetch (or not less than two-thirds of this).

Ragman: parchment document with many pendant seals.

Real: concerned with specific things (c.f. personal), or with land as distinct from chattels.

Receiver: one appointed to receive rents and profits of an estate.

Recognisance: formal acknowledgement of a debt or other obligation, usually with sureties and subject to special penalties for default.

Record: (a) authentic or official report of the proceedings in any cause coming before a court (i.e. according to the great 17th-century lawyer Coke, a court whose proceedings are formally enrolled and valid as evidence of fact, being also a court of the sovereign and having authority to fine or imprison), together with the judgement given therein, entered upon the roll of court and offering indisputable evidence of the matter in question; (b) copy of the material points, pleadings and issues between the defendant(s) and plaintiff(s) on a matter of law, constituting the case to be decided by the court; (c) account of some fact or event preserved in writing or other permanent form; (d) document, monument, etc., on which such an account is inscribed; (e) an authentic evidence.

Recorda: records of judicial proceedings for the recovery of crown debts.

Recordari facias (also loquelam): writ ordering a record to be made of proceedings in a court not of record.

Recovery: Restitution to a former right by the judgement of a court.

Recusant: one denying ecclesiastical supremacy of sovereign or refusing to attend the services of the established church.

Reeve: manorial official, commonly chosen from the villein tenants.

Regarder: supervisor of forests and president of a triennial court (court of regard) to enforce the forest laws.

Registers: volumes containing information and papers or copies of papers which have been accepted as evidence. A will may be entered in full, bonds, inventories and other documents attached may not be entered in the registers; affidavits on the other hand may well be.

Rejoinder: defendant's response to a plaintiff's replication.

Release: (a) a gift, discharge or renunciation of right of action; (b) conveyance of larger estate or reversion to one in possession. C.f. lease.

Relief: the dues payable to the lord by a freeholder upon entering his estate. This may take the form of knight's service or socage.

Remainder: the title to an estate dependent upon the end of the present tenancy. **Contingent remainder** means that the title to an estate is limited so that it depends upon a condition which may not occur.

Remembrancer: an official concerned with making and acting upon remembrances (memoranda, reminders).

Render in kind: payment in the form of specified goods.

Rent: a regular consideration payable as the value of service due for the tenancy of freehold or customary property for which it was a composition.

Rental: register of rents due, often naming tenants and/or tenements.

Rent-charge: rent charged on land, etc., and enforceable by a right of distress on default.

Renunciation: a person renounces or makes an act of renunciation by signing a document declining to apply for a grant of probate of letters of administration. A note to this effect usually appears in the Act Book. The person making such a renunciation is usually the executor of a will, a trustee or next of kin of the intestate, not wishing to take up the obligations.

Replevin: (action to enforce) redelivery of a pledge or thing taken in distress.

Replication, reply: pleading by a plaintiff in response to defendant's answer.

Report: statement of opinion on a matter referred by special inquiry.

Retinue: body of troops, etc., attached to a particular leader.

Rider: additional clause inserted after the completion of a document.

Right, writ of: writ initiating proceedings on a claim to land, etc., not based merely on possession.

Roll, rotulus: (a) a document consisting of several parchment membranes attached end to end (Chancery type) or rotulets all attached at the top (Plea Roll type); (b) single membrane or rotulet.

Royal Peculiar: the sovereign may have the right of presentation and personal ownership of a parish, a benefice or a royal chapel, which is usually outside the jurisdiction of a diocese and therefore for probate purposes is a testamentary peculiar.

Rule of court: (a) general regulation governing the conduct of court business; (b) order or direction, usually by a master (q.v.) as to procedure in a particular action.

Scavage: import duty or toll on goods of non-burgesses.

Scire facias: writ ordering a matter to be brought to the notice of someone, so that if he wishes, he may appear and defend his rights therein.

Scutage: feudal payment in commutation of knight service.

Secondary: official of the second rank, acting as a subordinate or deputy.

Seigneur: a feudal lord.

Seisin: possession of property, especially of real estate.

Seminary: training school of Roman Catholic priests, especially for missions.

Sentences: the opinions, determinations or final judgements, usually in respect of disputed wills, found in the Act Books, the Court Books and the registers.

Sequestration: temporary taking of property into official custody.

Serjeant-at-law: barrister of superior degree.

Serjeanty: feudal tenure of land by some service to the crown other than normal military or knight service, or land so held.

Sewer: for purposes of Commissions and Laws of Sewers, the term included rivers, public streams and ditches, etc.

Sheriff: originally 'shire-reeve', the principal agent of the crown in a county for administrative and financial purposes

Side-bar rule: judge's rule granted to an attorney upon a motion at the side-bar

Sign manual: hand-written signature, especially of the sovereign.

Signet: small personal seal, especially the king's 'secret seal' used by his secretary.

Significavit: writ ordering the detention of a person named in a bishop's certificate of excommunication.

Skippet: wooden or metal container for the preservation of a seal.

Socage: freehold land not subject to feudal service or incidents. This later came to mean, after the abolition of feudal tenure in 1661, the ordinary holding of an estate by inheritance.

Solicitor: originally a lawyer practising in the Court of Equity, equivalent to a common law attorney.

Spiritualities: ecclesiastical rights and revenues derived from tithes, oblations, etc., exempt from secular control. C.f. temporalities.

Stannary: privileged tin-mining area in Devon and Cornwall.

Staple: privileged market with monopoly for the sale of certain goods.

Statute Staple: authority empowering a major and constables of a staple to take and seal recognisance or obligations of debts.

Sub-infeudation: granting of lands by one person in the feudal hierarchy to another of lower rank; the lands to be held under the same terms as those pertaining to the original holder.

Sub pena, subpoena: writ ordering appearance in court 'under a penalty' specified.

Subsidy: a grant of money made by Parliament to a sovereign for a specific purpose, and raised by a tax levied according to the lands held, etc.

Supersedeas: writ ordering a stay of court proceedings.

Supplicavit: writs issued at the instance of petitioners for taking securities from persons alleged to be threatening them.

Surrogate: a substitute; in ecclesiastical matters, a deputy appointed by the ecclesiastical court to act on its behalf.

Swainmote, swanimote: triannual forest court, especially concerned with the pasturing of pigs, etc.

Tallage: arbitrary impost, especially on lands held by unfree tenants and ancient demesne of crown.

Tally: (a) piece of wood scored across with notches for the items of an account and then split into halves of which each party concerned kept one; (b) account so kept.

Taxing: assessment of costs.

Teller: one who 'tells' (counts out) money.

Temporalities: secular possessions, land etc., of an ecclesiastical dignitary or body, held by the crown during a vacancy; c.f. spiritualities.

Tenant: the occupier of lands or tenements of another who holds possessed of real estate by right.

Tenant-in-chief: feudal tenant holding direct from the crown without the imposition of a mesne tenant.

Tenements: the holding of property, land, dwelling(s), customary estate.

Tenth, clerical: levied for the recovery of the Holy Land.

Term: (a) specified duration of a tenancy, etc.; (b) one of the four periods of the year - c.f. *Handbook of Dates*, Royal Historical Society, 1948, p. 65 - available for judicial business.

Terrae Captae: lands taken into the king's hand.

Terrae Datae: lands alienated by the crown.

Terrier: register or survey of land, usually indicating boundaries and tenures.

Testament: *see* will.

Thanage: the tenure by which lands were held by a thane.

Thane, thegn: one who held lands of the king or other superior by military service.

Tidewaiters: *see* waiters.

Tithe: originally a tenth of the produce of land and livestock, payable to the rector (ecclesiastical or lay) for the maintenance of a parish priest; later normally commuted by agreement of award.

Title: right to land or other property, with reference to the mode of acquisition and the power of transfer.

Toll: payment levied usually for passage or for use of market.

Tontine: annuity increasing annually as the number of subscribers is diminished by death.

Tourn: law-hundred, major (biannual) session of a hundred court, under the presidency of a sheriff.

Township: vill, local community, usually smaller than a town and sometimes coincident with parish.

Trailbaston: sessions held by justices throughout the country.

Transportation of felons: sending overseas to serve a sentence of hard labour.

Traverse: formal denial or dispute of inquisition, etc.

Treasure trove: money or precious metal of unknown ownership found hidden.

Trespass: (a) breach of criminal law other than treason or felony; (b) civil wrong actionable by writ to recover damages.

Trust: obligation enforceable in equity incumbent on one having an interest in property for the benefit of another.

Tuition: guardianship over orphaned minors, usually under the age of 15 in respect of boys, and of 13 in the case of girls.

Tunnage: duty of so much a tun on wine.

Unproven wills: these are sometimes called *re-infecta wills*. Wills for which no grant of probate under the seal of the court has been made may be registered though they are unprobated. Contrariwise, wills may have been proved but not entered into the registers. The reasons for this may be many, including the failure of the executor to pay the fees for registration of probate. The will is none the less valid.

Ulnage: (a) official measurement and inspection of woollen cloth; (b) fee for such measurement.

Venire papers: writs directing empanelment of jurors, with the returns.

Venison: hunting or flesh of beasts protected by game laws, especially deer or other large game.

Verderer: forest official appointed to protect growing trees and shrubs (*vert*) and venison.

Verdict: decision of jury on issue submitted to them.

Verge: a distance of 12 miles round the royal residence.

Vice-admiral: in admiralty court jurisdiction the deputy of the Lord High Admiral within a specified district.

Victualler: supplier of food to the public, ships or troops.

Vidimus: *see* inspeximus.

View: inspection of property in a dispute, of work in progress or of account not yet ready for audit.

Vill: *see* township.

Virgate: the customary division of land (from 10 to 15 acres in Sussex to twice as much elsewhere), called 'bovate' in the North.

Visitation: inspection of a church or religious house, etc., by a bishop or his representative.

Voucher: document serving as a warrant or receipt for payment.

Voucher to Warranty: request by a grantee or his heir that the grantor or his heir should be summoned to defend the former's title.

Waiters: customs officers, comprising tide-waiters who boarded ships before landing and land-waiters or searchers who inspected them after landing.

Wapentake: division of a county in the Danelaw, corresponding to a hundred.

Ward: (a) a minor in the keeping of a guardian, especially a feudal overlord; (b) obligation to aid in the defence of a castle; (c) division of a city or town, especially London, or of a county (northern).

Wardmote: court held in each of the London wards.

Wardrobe: storage and expenditure department of the royal household, with offshoots including the Great Wardrobe (for bulk stores, mainly military) and the Privy Wardrobe.

Wardship: the right of the lord to take custody of the heir of one of his tenants during the minority of the child and to enjoy the profits of the estate.

Warrant: document serving as an authority for payment, grant, appointment or other act.

Warranty: undertaking by the grantor of land, etc., on behalf of himself and his heirs, to defend the title of the grantee and his heirs or assigns.

Warren, right of: liberty of preserving and hunting small game within a specified area.

Waste: (a) uncultivated land; (b) damage to buildings, timber, etc., by a tenant for life or for a term of years.

Will: a final written statement by which a person regulates the disposition of property and rights at his decease (formerly, concerned with land only as distinct from the testament, which dealt with goods).

Woodward: forest officer in charge of growing timber.

Writ, breve: sealed document conveying a formal command of the crown or of a court.

Yeoman: (a) servant in a royal or noble household; (b) a free-holding farmer who may be a member of a mounted group of soldiery of this rank.

BIBLIOGRAPHY

1. *USEFUL BOOKS AND ARTICLES*

ABBOTT, JOHN PATRICK, *Family Patterns: A Personal Experience of Genealogy* (1971)

ADDINGTON, A.C., *The Royal House of Stuart* (3 vols., 1976)

ANDERSON, J.P., *The Book of British Topography* (1881)

'Archives and Manuscripts in Libraries', *Library Association Record*, vol. 59, 1957, pp. 238-9)

ARMYTAGE, G.J., (ed.), 'Allegations for Marriage Licences...1543-1869' (extracted by J.L. Chester, *Harleian Society* vol. 24, 1886)

BANKS, CHARLES EDWARD, *The English Ancestry and Homes of the Pilgrim Fathers* (1970)

BANKS, T.C., *Dormant and extinct Baronies of England* (4 vols., 1807-37)

BARDSLEY, CHARLES WAREING, *A Dictionary of English and Welsh Surnames with special American instances* (1968)

BARLEY, M.W., *The English Farmhouse and Cottage* (1961)

Bartholomew's Gazetteer of Britain (1977)

BARROW, G.B., *The Genealogist's Guide* (1977)

BEATSON, R., *Political Index to the Histories of Great Britain and Ireland* (3 vols., 3rd edn. 1806)

BENSON, J., 'Feudal Age Pedigrees', *The Genealogist's Magazine*, vol. 10 no. 1, March 1947, p. 10)

BERESFORD, M.W., *Lay Subsidies, 1290-1334; post 1334; and Poll Taxes, 1377, 1379 and 1381* (1963)

BERNAU, C.A., *Exchequer Deponents, 1559-1695* (3 vols., 1916-18)

BESTERMANN, THEODORE, *World Bibliography of Bibliographies* (4th edn., 1965-6)

BICKLEY, F.B., and ELLIS, H.J., *Index to the Charters and Rolls in the Department of Manuscripts, British Museum, London* (1900)

BLAND, D.S., 'The Records of the Inns of Court: a bibliographical aid' (*Amateur Historian*, vol. 5, no. 2, 1962, p. 77)

BLOOM, J. HARVEY, 'Genealogical Data before the Black Death' (*Genealogist's Magazine*, vol. 6 no. 10, June 1934, p. 471)

BLOOM, J. HARVEY, and JAMES, R.R., *Medical practitioners in the Diocese of London...1529-1725* (1935)

BOND, M.F., *Guide to the Records of Parliament* (1971)

BOND, M.F., *The Records of Parliament* (1964)

BOUTELL, C., *English Heraldry* (ed. J. Brooke-Little, new edn. 1983)

BOYER, C., *Ship Passenger Lists: National and New England, 1600-1825* (1977)

BOYER, C., *Ship Passenger Lists: New York and New Jersey, 1600-1825* (1981)

BOYER, C., *Ship Passenger Lists: Pennsylvania and Delaware, 1641-1825* (1980)

BOYER, C., *Ship Passenger Lists: The Southern United States, 1538-1825* (1979)

BRADSHAW, F., 'The Lay Subsidies of 1296' (*Archaeologica Aeliana*, 3rd series vol. 13, 1916, pp.180-302)

BRIDGER, CHARLES, *An Index to Printed Pedigrees contained in county and local histories, the Heralds' Visitations, etc.* (1891-5, reprinted 1969)

BRINKWORTH, E.R.C., 'The Study and Use of Archdeacon's Court Records' (*Transactions of the Royal Historical Society*, 1942)

British National Archives Publications of the Public Record Office, Public Record Office (Belfast), Scottish Record Office and House of Lords Record Office (Her Majesty's Stationery Office, 1973 onwards; see *Government Publications Sectional List no. 24*)

British Records Association, reports from the Committees of: No. 1, General Report ... on the classification of English Archives (1936); No. 2, Classified List of the Varieties of Document which may be found in Parish Archives (1936); No. 3, Archives of Religious and Ecclesiastical Bodies and Organisations other than the Church of England (1936); No. 5, List of Record Repositories in Great Britain (1956)

Burke's Colonial Gentry (1970)

Burke's Commoners (reprinted 1977)

Burke's Extinct Baronetcies (revised edn. 1969)

Burke's Family Records (1897, reprinted 1965)

Burke's Family Index (reprinted 1976)

Burke's General Armory of England, Scotland, Ireland and Wales (1884)

Burke's Guide to the Royal Family (1973)

Burke's Irish Family Records (5th edn., 1975-6)

Burke's Introduction to Irish Ancestry (1976)

Burke's Landed Gentry, Peerage and Baronetage (1826, reprinted 1975)

Burke's Presidential Families of the United States of America (1975)

Burke's Royal Families of the World (2 vols., 1977)

BURN, J.S., *The History of Parish Registers* (1862, reprinted 1976)

Calendar of Entries in the Papal Registers relating to Great Britain and Ireland: papal letters (Public Record Office, 13 vols., 1893-1955)

Calendar of Entries in the Papal Registers relating to Great Britain and Ireland: petitions to the Pope: vol. 1, 1342-1419 (ed. W.H. Bliss, Public Record Office, 1896)

CAM, HELEN, 'Pedigrees of Villeins and Freemen in the 13th century' (*Genealogist's Magazine*, vol. 6, Sept. 1933, p. 299)

CAMP, A.J., *Wills and their Whereabouts* (1974)

CAMP, A.J., *Tracing your Ancestors* (1979)

Catalogue of Directories and Poll Books at the Society of Genealogists (1974 edn.)

CAMPLING, A., 'Sources of Genealogical Research before 1349' (?, vol. 7, June 1935, p. 61)

CAPPELLI, ADRIANO, *Dizionario di abbreviature latine ed. Italiano* (2nd edn. 1912)

CARSON, I.A. RITCHIE, *The Ecclesiastical Courts of York* (1950)

CARTER, G., *Outlines of English History* (1970)

CAUSTON, H.K.S., *Rights of Heirship, or, the Doctrine of Descents and Consanguinity as applied by the Law of England to Real Property, Titular Honours, Coat Armour, etc.* (1842)

CHALLEN, W.H., 'The Records of the City of London' (*Genealogist's Magazine*, vol. 6, Sept. 1934, p. 503)

CHAPLAIS, PIERRE, *English Royal Documents: King John - Henry VI, 1199-1461* (1971)

CHENEY, C.R., *Handbook of Dates for Students of English History* (Royal Historical Society, 1945, reprinted 1965)

CIRKET, A.F., 'English Wills, 1498-1526' (*Bedfordshire Historical Record Society*, vol. 37, 1957)
CLARK, G.K., *Guide for Research Students working on Historical Subjects* (1968 edn.)
CLARK, H., *An Introduction to Heraldry*
CLAY, J.W., *Extinct and Dormant Peerages of the Northern Counties of England, Yorkshire, Westmorland, Lancaster* (1913)
COKAYNE, GEORGE EDWARD, et al., (eds.), *The Complete Peerage* (13 vols., new edn. revised by V. Gibbs, 1910-59)
COKAYNE, GEORGE EDWARD, et al., (eds.), *The Complete Baronetage* (6 vols, 1900-1909)
COLEMAN, J., *General Index to Printed Pedigrees* (1866)
COLLIS, IVOR P., 'Leases for a term of years determinate with lives' (*Journal of the Society of Archivists*, vol. 1, no. 6, Oct. 1957)
COLWELL, S., *The Family History Book; A Guide to Tracing your Ancestors* (1980)
COOKE, W.H., (ed.), *Students admitted to the Inner Temple, 1547-1660* (1878)
COPE, S.T., 'Heraldry, flags and seals: a select bibliography with annotations, covering the period 1920 to 1945' (*Journal of Documentation*, vol. 4, 1948)
CORNWALL, JULIAN, *How to read Old Title Deeds, XVI-XIX centuries* (1964)
CORNWALL, JULIAN, 'A Tudor Domesday: the Musters of 1522' (*Journal of the Society of Archivists*, vol. 3, no. 1, April 1965)
COSTER, J., *Oxford Men and their Colleges* (1893)
COX, J.C., and PADFIELD, T., *Tracing your Ancestors in the Public Record Office* (1981)
COX, J.C., *Churchwardens' Accounts* (1913)
COX, J.C., *Parish Registers of England* (1910)
CRASTER, H.H.E., *The Western Manuscripts of the Bodleian Library* (1921)
CUNNINGHAM, W., *Alien Immigrants to England* (1897, reprinted 1969)
CURRER-BRIGGS, NOEL, *Debrett's Family Historian: a Guide to Tracing your Ancestors* (1981)
CURRER-BRIGGS, NOEL, *English Adventurers and Virginian Settlers* (3 vols., 1969)
CURRER-BRIGGS, NOEL, *English Adventurers and Colonial Settlers* (1971)
CURRER-BRIGGS, NOEL, *A Handbook of British Family History* (1979)
Debrett's Peerage, Baronetage, Knightage and Companionage (1971)
Debrett's Peerage and Baronetage, with Her Majesty's Warrant Holders (1980)
DANIELL, E.R., *Chancery Practice and Forms* (8th edn. ed. by S.E. Williams and F. Guthrie-Smith, 1914)
DAVIES, J.C., 'Ecclesiastical and Palatinate Archives at the Prior's Diocesan and Archidiaconal Kitchen, Durham' (*Journal of the Society of Archivists*, vol. 1, no. 7, April 1958, p. 185)
Descriptive Catalogue of Ancient Deeds in the Public Record Office (6 vols., 1890-1915)
DAWSON, G.E., and KENNEDY-SKIPTON, L., *Elizabethan Handwriting, 1500-1650* (1968)
DENHOLM-YOUNG, N., *Handwriting in England and Wales* (1954)
DIBBEN, A.A., *Title Deeds* (1968)
DOANE, G.H., *Searching for your Ancestors: the How and Why of Genealogy* (1968)
DOYLE, J.W.E., *Official Baronage of England* (3 vols., 1886)
DU BOULAY, F. R.H., *Handlist of Medieval Ecclesiastical Terms* (Standing Conference for Local History, 1952)

DUGDALE, W., *The Baronage of England* (2 vols., 1675-6)

DOYLE, JAMES, *The Official Baronetage of England* (3 vols., 1886)

ELLIS, G., *Earldoms in Fee* (1963)

ELMHURST, E.M., 'Merchants' Marks' (*Harleian Society* vol. 108, 1959)

ELVIN, C.N., *A Dictionary of Heraldry* (1969 reprint of 1889 edn.)

ELVIN, C.N., *A Handbook of Mottoes borne by the Nobility and Gentry* (1971)

EMMISON, F.G., *Archives and Local History* (1974)

EMMISON, F.G., *Introduction to Archives* (1977)

EMMISON, F.G., and HUMPHREYS, D.W., *Local History for Students* (1965)

EMMISON, F.G., *How to Read Local Archives, 1550-1700* (Historical Association, 1967)

English Local History Handlist (National Council for Social Service)

ERNLE, ROWLAND E. PROTHERO, *English Farming Past and Present* (6th edn. with Introduction by G.E. Fussell and O.R. McGregor, 1961)

Fairbairn's Book of Crests of the Families of Great Britain and Ireland (4th edn. 1905)

FALLEY, M.D., *Irish and Scotch-Irish Ancestral Research* (2 vols., 1962)

FILBY, P.W., and MEYER, M., *Passenger and Immigration Lists Index* (3 vols., 1981; *Bibliography*, 1981; *First Supplement*, 1982)

FILBY, P.W., *American and British Genealogy and Heraldry* (1970)

FINBERG, H.P.R., *The Local Historian and his Theme* (1952)

FINBERG, H.P.R., and SKIPP, V.H.T., *Local History: objective and pursuit* (1967)

FINES, J., 'Documents in the Public Record Office: 3, the Early Chancery Proceedings' (*Amateur Historian*, vol. 6, no. 8, Summer 1965)

FLETCHER, R.J., (ed.), *Pension Book of Gray's Inn, 1569-1800* (2 vols., 1901-10)

FFOLIOT, ROSEMARY, *A Simple Guide to Irish Genealogy* (3rd revised edn., 1967)

FORSTER, J., *The Baronage and Knightage of England* (1892)

FOSTER, J., (ed.), *Alumni Oxonienses, 1500-1886* (8 vols., 1887-92)

FOSTER, J., (ed.), *London Marriage Licences, 1521-1869* (1887)

FOSTER, J., (ed.), *Register of Gray's Inn Admissions, 1521-1889* (1889)

FOWLER, R.C., *Episcopal Registers of England and Wales* (Society for the Propagation of Christian Knowledge, 1918)

FOX-DAVIES, A.C, *Armorial Families* (1929, reprinted 1974)

FRY, E.A., 'Index of Chancery Proceedings (Reynardson's Division), preserved in the Public Record Office A.D. 1649-1714' (*British Record Society Index Library*, vols. 29, 32, 1903-4)

FURNIVALL, F.J., 'The fifty earliest wills in the Court of Probate, 1387-1439' copied and edited from the original registers in Somerset House, 1882 (*Early English Text Society*, vol. 78, 1882, reprinted 1964)

GALBRAITH, V.H., *An Introduction to the Use of Public Records* (1952)

GALBRAITH, V.H., *Studies in the Public Records* (1948)

GALBRAITH, V.H., *The Making of Domesday Book* (1961)

GANDY, M., *My Ancestor was Jewish: How can I find out more about him?* (1982)

GARDNER, D.E., and SMITH, F., *Immigrants to America appearing in English records* (1976)

GARRETT, R.E.F., *Chancery and Other Legal Proceedings* (1968)

GATFIELD, G.A., *Guide to Heraldry and Genealogy* (1892, reprinted 1966)

GATFIELD, G., *Guide to Printed Books and Manuscripts relating to English and Foreign Heraldry and Genealogy* (1892)

GIBSON, J.S.W., *Wills and Where to Find Them* (1974)

GIBSON, J.S.W., *Bishops' Transcripts and Marriage Licences; Bonds and Allegations. A Guide to their Location and Indexes* (1983)

GIBSON, J.S.W., *Census Indexes and Indexing* (1983)

GIBSON, J.S.W., *Marriage, Census and other Indexes for Family Historians* (1984, reprinted 1985)

GIBSON, J.S.W., *Census Returns, 1841, 1851, 1861, 1871, and 1881 on Microfilm: A Directory of Local Holdings* (1983)

GIBSON, J.S.W., *Record Offices: How to Find Them* (1983)

GIBSON, J.S.W., *A Simplified Guide to Probate Jurisdictions: Where to Look for Wills* (1983)

GIBSON, J.S.W., *Land Tax Assessments, c. 1690-1950* (1983)

GIBSON, J.S.W., *Quarter Sessions Records: a Select List for Family Historians* (1982)

GIBSON, J.S.W., *Where to find the International Genealogists Index* (forthcoming)

GIBSON, J.S.W., *Hearth Tax Returns and other late Stuart Tax Lists* (1984)

GILLETT, E., 'Proofs of Age' (*Amateur Historian*, vol. 5, p. 224)

GILSON, J.P., *A Student's Guide to the Manuscripts of the British Museum* (Society for the Promotion of Christian Knowledge, Helps for the Student of History, no. 31, 1920)

GIVEN-WILSON, C. and CURTEIS, A., *Royal Bastards of Medieval England* (1984)

GLENCROSS, R.M., *Administrations in the Prerogative Court of Canterbury, 1559-1580* (2 vols., 1912-7)

GLOVER, F.R., and HARRIS, R.W., *Latin for Historians* (3rd edn., 1963)

GOODER, E.A., *Latin for Local History* (1961)

GOMME, G.L., *Index of Archaeological Papers, 1665-1890*

GOUGH, J., *Sepulchral Monuments* (1780-96)

GRAHAM, N.H., *Genealogist's Consolidated Guide to Parish Registers in the Inner London Area, 1538-1837* (1976)

GRAHAM, N.H., *Genealogist's Consolidated Guide to Parish Registers in the Outer London Area, 1538-1837* (1977)

GRAHAM, N.H., *Genealogist's Consolidated Guide to Nonconformist and Foreign Registers, Copies and Indexes in the Inner London Area, 1538-1837* (1980)

GREEN, E., *Preparations in Somerset against the Armada* (1888)

GREEN, J.J., *Quaker Records* (1894)

GRIEVE, HILDA E.P., *Examples of English Handwriting, 1150-1750* (14th impression, 1974)

GRIGG, D.B., 'A Source of Landownership: the Land Tax Returns' (*Amateur Historian*, vol. 6, no. 5, 1964)

GROSS, C., *Sources and Literature of English History from the Earliest Times to about 1485* (2nd edn., 1915)

Guide to the British Museum (1968)

Guide to the Contents of the Public Record Office (3 vols., 1963-8)

GUPPY, HENRY BROUGHAM, *Homes of Family Names in Great Britain* (1968)

HADYN, J.T., *Book of Dignitaries* (1904)

HALL, H., *Repertory of British Archives, compiled ... for the Royal Historical Society* (1920)

HALL, H., *Select Bibliography for the Study, Sources and Literature of English medieval economic history* (1914)

HALL, W., *Canting and Allusive Arms of England and Wales* (1966)
HALLIWELL, J.O., *Dictionary of Archaic and Provincial Words* (2 vols., 1868)
HAMILTON-EDWARDS, GERALD, *In Search of Ancestry* (1983 edn.)
HAMILTON-EDWARDS, GERALD, *In Search of Army Ancestry* (1978)
HAMILTON-EDWARDS, GERALD, *In Search of Scottish Ancestry* (1983 edn.)
'Handlist of sources for Heralds' Visitation Pedigrees' (*Family History*, vol. 1, 1962)
Handbook on Irish Genealogy (1973)
HARLEY, J.B., 'The Hundred Rolls of 1279' (*Amateur Historian*, vol. 5, no. 1, 1961)
HARRIS, P.V., 'Glossary of Terms from Parochial Records' (*Amateur Historian*, vol. 1, no. 4, 1953, pp. 122-4)
HARVEY, R., *Genealogy for Librarians* (1983)
HASLAM, G.E., (ed.), *Manchester Public Libraries, Reference Library, Subject Catalogue, section 929, Genealogy* (3 parts, Manchester Library Committee, 1956-7)
HECTOR, L.C., *The Handwriting of English Documents* (reprinted 1980)
HECTOR, L.C., 'Genealogy in the Public Records' (*Genealogist's Magazine*, vol. 8, 1938, pp. 57-68)
HEIM, ARCHBISHOP B.B., *Heraldry in the Catholic Church* (1978)
HILTON, R.H., 'Short Glossary of Manorial Terms' (*Amateur Historian*, vol. 3, 1953, p.86)
HOLLAENDER, A.E.J., 'Ecclesiastical Records transferred to the Guildhall Library from Somerset House' (*Transactions of the London and Middlesex Archaeological Society*, vol. 21, 1959)
HOLMES, FRANK R., *Directory of the Ancestral Heads of New England Families, 1620-1700* (1974)
HONE, N.J., *The Manor and Manorial Records* (1925)
HOPWOOD, C.H., *Calendar of the Middle Temple Records* (1903)
HOSKINS, W.G., 'Yeoman Families and their Pedigrees' (*Transactions of the Leicestershire Archaeological Society*, vol. 23, part 1, 1947)
HOSKINS, W.G., 'The Genealogical Value of the Subsidies of 1327 and 1332' (*Devon and Cornwall Notes and Queries*, vol. 12, no. 7, July 1943, pp. 169-172)
HOSKINS, W.G., *Local History in England* (1973)
HOUSE, W.H., 'The dating of old records' (*Transactions of the Radnorshire Society*, vol. 32, 1962)
HOWARD, J.J., and CRISP, F.A., (eds.), *Visitations of England and Wales* (1893-1921)
HUBBACK, J., *A Treatise on the Evidence of Succession to Real and Personal Property and Peerages* (1844)
HUDSON, W., 'The Three Earliest Subsidies in 1296, 1327 and 1332' (*Sussex Record Society*, vol. 10, 1910)
HUMPHERY-SMITH, C.R., *The Phillimore Atlas and Index of Parish Registers* (1984)
HUMPHERY-SMITH, C.R., 'Marriage Licences, Bonds, and Allegations' (*Family History*, vol. 5, no. 25, n.s. 1, 1967)
HUMPHERY-SMITH, C.R., *General Armory Two* (1978)
HUMPHERY-SMITH, C.R., *Anglo-Norman Armory* (1978)

HUMPHERY-SMITH, C.R., 'Genealogy from Manorial Records' (*Genealogist's Magazine*, vol. 14, no. 1, March 1963)
HUMPHERY-SMITH, C.R., *Introduction to Medieval Genealogy* (1975)
HUMPHERY-SMITH, C.R., *Introducing Family History* (1983 edn.)
HUMPHERY-SMITH, C.R., *The Family History Book* (1967)
HUMPHERY-SMITH, C.R., *London's Right Road for the Study of Heraldry* (1964)
HUNTER, J., 'Familiae Minorum Gentium' (ed. J.W. Clay, *Harleian Society*, vols. 37-40, 1894-6)
HUNTER, J., 'Hunter's Pedigrees: A Continuation of Familiae Minorum Gentium' (ed. J.W. Walker, *Harleian Society*, vol. 88, 1936)
HUNTER, REVD. J., *The Great Rolls of Pipe, 1155-8*
HUTCHINSON, J., *Catalogue of the Notable Middle Templars, 1501-1901* (1902)
INGPEN, A.R., *Middle Temple Bench Book: being a register of Benchers...from the earliest times to the present time* (1912)
INSTITUTE OF HISTORICAL RESEARCH, *Guide to the Accessibility of Local Records of England and Wales*: part 1, records of counties, boroughs, dioceses, cathedrals, archdeaconries and probate offices; part 2, records of the Inns of Court, collegiate churches, local educational foundations, repositories approved by the Master of the Rolls and local societies (1982-4)
INSTITUTE OF HISTORICAL RESEARCH, *Guide to the Victoria County History* (1912)
'Introduction to the Study of the Pipe Rolls' (*Pipe Roll Society*, 1884)
IREDALE, DAVID, *Enjoying Archives* (1973, new edn. 1985)
IREDALE, DAVID, *Local History Research and Writing* (1980, new edn. 1985)
IREDALE, DAVID, *Discovering your Family Tree* (1970)
INDERWICK, F.A., and ROBERTS, R.A., (eds.), *Calendar of Inner Temple Records, 1505-1750* (4 vols., 1896-1934)
JACOBS, P.M., *Registers of the universities, schools and colleges of Great Britain and Ireland* (Institute of Historical Research, 1964)
JARVIS, R.C., 'Records of Customs and Excise Services' (*Genealogist's Magazine*, vol. 10, no. 76, Sept. 1948, p. 219)
JENKINS, C., *Ecclesiastical Records* (Historical Association, 1920)
JENKINSON, C. HILARY, *The Later Court Hands in England* (1927)
JENKINSON, C.HILARY, and JOHNSON, C., *English Court Hand, A.D. 1066-1500* (2 vols., 1915)
JOHNSON, G.D., 'Legal Terms and Phrases' (*Amateur Historian*, vol. 3, 1957-8, p. 249)
JOHNSON, W. BRANCH, 'Notes before reading Court Rolls' (*Amateur Historian*, vol. 4, no. 3, 1959)
JORDAN, W.K., *Charities of Rural England, 1480-1660* (1961)
JUDGE, C.B., *Specimens of 16th-century English Handwriting* (1935)
KAMINKOW, M.J., *New Bibliography of British Genealogy from Booksellers' Catalogues* (1965)
KAMINKOW, M.J., *Genealogies in the Library of Congress Bibliography* (2 vols., 1972)
KELHAM, R.E., *Anglo-Norman Dictionary* (1779)
KELLAWAY, W., 'Record Publications of Societies' (*Archaeologia*, vol. 7 (46), 1965)
A Key to the Parishes included in Boyd's Marriage Index (Genealogical Society of Utah)

KNOCKER, HERBERT W., 'Manorial Records' (*Genealogist's Magazine*, vol. 6, no. 3, Sept. 1932, p. 92)

KNOWLES, D., *The Monastic Order in England* (3 vols., 1962)

LANE, H.M., *Royal Daughters of England, with Genealogical Tables of the Royal Family* (1910-1)

LATHAM, R.E., *Revised Medieval Latin Word-List* (1965)

List of Works relating to Records (H.M.S.O.)

LAWRANCE, H., 'Heraldry from Military Monuments before 1350 in England and Wales' (*Harleian Society*, vol. 98, 1946)

LEADAM, I.S., (ed.), *Domesday of Inclosures, 1517-8* (1898)

LEARY, REV. WILLIAM, *My Ancestor was a Methodist: How can I find out more about him?* (1982)

LE NEVE, J., 'Pedigrees of Knights' (ed. G.W. Marshall, *Harleian Society* vol. 8, 1873)

LEVETT, A.E., *Studies in Manorial History* (1963)

List of Accessions to Repositories (National Register of Archives, 1966)

'List of depositories authorised by the Master of the Rolls to receive Manorial Records'(*Bulletin of the British Record Society*, vol. 1, 1924)

LEWIS, S., *A Topographical Dictionary of England* (4 vols. and atlas vol, 5th edn., 1842

LEWIS, S., *A Topographical Dictionary of Wales* (2 vols., 2nd edn., 1838)

LEWIS, S., *A Topographical Dictionary of Scotland* (2 vols., supp. vol., map, 1847)

LEWIS, S., *A Topographical Dictionary of Ireland* (2 vols., plus areas vol., 1837)

LITTLE, R.H., 'Military History from Local History Sources' (*Amateur Historian*, vol. 7, no. 4)

LITTLEDALE, W.A., 'A Collection of Miscellaneous Grants, Crests, Confirmations, Augmentations and Exemplifications of Arms in the MSS preserved in the British Museum, Ashmolean Library, Queen's College Oxford, and elsewhere' (*Harleian Society*, vols. 76, 77, 1925-6)

LOYD, L.C., 'Origins of some Anglo-Norman families' (ed. C.T. Clay and D.C. Douglas, *Harleian Society* vol. 103, 1951, reprinted 1980)

McFARLANE, A., *Guide to English Historical Records* (1963)

McKAY, D.A., 'The dating of records' (*Amateur Historian*, vol. 2, no. 6, June/July 1955)

MacKINNON OF DUNAKIN, C., *The Observer's Book of Heraldry* (1966)

McMICHAEL, N.H., 'A 14th-century pedigree' (*Genealogist's Magazine*, vol. 12, no. 16, Dec. 1958)

McNAUGHTON, A., *The Book of Kings: A Royal Genealogy* (1974)

MADAN, S., *Summary Catalogue of Western Manuscripts in the Bodleian Library at Oxford* (7 vols., 1895-1953)

MAITLAND, F.W., 'Select Pleas in Manorial and other Seigneurial Courts' (*Selden Society*, vol. 1, 1889)

MANDER, M., *Tracing Your Ancestors* (1976)

MARKS, R., and PAYNE, A., *British Heraldry from its Origins to c. 1800* (1980)

MARSHALL, G.W., *Handbook to the Ancient Courts of Probate and Depositories of Wills* (2nd edn., 1895)

MARSHALL, G.W., (ed.), 'Calendar of Wills in Lambeth Palace Library, 1313-1616' (*The Genealogist*, vols. 5-6, 1881-2)

MARSHALL, G.W., (ed.), 'Calendar of Lambeth Administrations, 1351-1616' (*The Genealogist*, vol. 7, n.s. 1, 1883-4)
MARSHALL, G.W., *The Genealogist's Guide* (1903 edn. reprinted 1973)
MARSHALL, G.W., 'Index to Hunter's *Familiae Minorum Gentium*' (*The Genealogist*, n.s. vol. 6, 1889)
MARSHALL, L.M., 'Levying of the Hearth Tax, 1662-88' (*English Historical Review*, vol. 51, 1936)
MARTIN, C. TRICE, *The Record Interpreter* (1910, reprinted 1982)
MARTIN, C.TRICE, *Minutes of Parliament of the Middle Temple, 1501-1703* (1904-5)
MARTIN, G.H., 'The origin of borough records' (*Journal of the Society of Archivists*, vol. 2, no. 4, Oct. 1961, p. 147)
MASSEY, R.W., *A List of Parishes in Boyd's Marriage Index* (1974)
MASSUE, M.H., [The Marquis de Ruvigny & Raineval], *The Jacobite Peerage: Baronetage, Knightage and Grants of Honour* (1904, reprinted 1974)
Masters of the Bench 1450-1883; and Masters of the Inner Temple 1540-1883 and Treasurers 1505-1901 (2 vols., 1883-1901)
MATTHEWS, C.J., *Your Family History and how to discover it* (1976)
Members of Parliament, 1213-1874 (4 vols., Her Majesty's Stationery Office, 1878-91)
MERRIMAN, R.D., 'Naval Records' (*Genealogist's Magazine*, vol. 10, no. 4, 1947)
MEYER, M., and FILBY, P.W., *Passenger and Immigration Lists Index* (1981); *Bibliography* (1981); *Supplement* (1982)
MONCRIEFFE, SIR IAIN OF THAT ILK, and POTTINGER, DON, *Simple Heraldry Cheerfully Explained* (1979)
MOOR, C., (ed.), 'Knights of Edward I' (*Harleian Society*, vols. 80-4, 1929-32)
MOORE, M.F., *Two select bibliographies of medieval historical study* (1912)
MOULTON, H.R., *Paleography, Genealogy and Topography: a sale catalogue of deeds, etc.* (1930)
MOULTON, H.R., *Index to nearly 30,000 surnames in a sale catalogue of deeds, etc.* (1937)
MULLINS, E.L.C., *Guide to the Historical Publications of the Societies of England and Wales* (1901-33)
MULLINS, E.L.C., *Texts and Calendars: an analytical guide to serial publications* (Royal Historical Society Guides and Handbooks, no. 7, 1958, 2nd edition 1982)
MUNBY, L.M., *Short Guide to Records* (Historical Association, 1972)
National Index of Parish Registers: Vol. 1, Sources of Births, Marriages and Deaths before 1837 (1976 edn.); Vol. 2, Sources for Nonconformist Genealogy and Family History (1973); Vol. 3, Sources for Roman Catholic and Jewish Genealogy and Family History (1974); Vol. 4, South East England: Kent, Surrey, Sussex (1980); Vol. 5, South Midlands and Welsh Borders (1966, reprinted 1976); Vol. 6, North Midlands: part i, Staffordshire (1982); Vol. 7, Norfolk, Suffolk and Cambridgeshire (1983); Vol. 11, Durham and Northumberland: part i (1979); Vol. 12, Sources for Scottish Genealogy and Family History (1971)
NEUBECKER, O., *A Guide to Heraldry* (1981)
NEWTON, K.C., *Medieval Local Records* (1971)

NEWTON, K.C., 'Reading medieval local records' (*Amateur Historian*, vol. 3, no. 2, 1956-7)

O'HART, J., *The Irish and Anglo-Irish Landed Gentry* (1884)

Original Parish Registers in Record Offices and Libraries (1975: 1st supplement, 1976; 2nd supplement, 1978; 3rd supplement, 1980; 4th supplement, 1982)

Parish Register Copies: Part 1, the Society of Genealogists' Collection (1982)

Parish Register Copies: Part 2, other than the Society of Genealogists' Collection (1974)

Oxford Honours, 1220-1894, being an alphabetical register of distinctions conferred (1894)

OWEN, D.M., *The Records of the Established Church in England, excluding parochial records* (British Records Association, 1970)

PALGRAVE-MOORE, P., *How to Record Your Family Tree* (1979)

PAPWORTH, J. W. and MORANT, A. W., *Ordinary of British Armorials* (1977 facsimile of 1847 edn.)

PARKES, M.B., *English Cursive Bookhands 1250-1500* (1979)

PARRY, C.J., *Catalogue of Baronetage Creations* (1964)

PHILBY, P.W., *American and British Genealogy and Heraldry: a bibliography* (1974)

PHILLIMORE, W.P.W., *Indexes to Irish Wills* (1940)

PHILLIMORE, W.P.W., and FRY, E.A., (eds.), 'Calendar of Chancery Proceedings, bills and answers filed in the reign of King Charles I' (*British Record Society Index Library*, vols. 2, 5, 6, 14, 1889-96)

PHILLIMORE, W.P.W. and FRY, E.A., (eds.), 'Coram rege pleas of the Court of King's Bench, 25 Edward I 1297' (*British Record Society Index Library*, vol. 19, 1898)

PHILLIMORE, W.P.W., *How to write the History of a Family* (1887; supplement 1896)

PHILLIMORE, W.P.W. and FRY, E.A., (eds.), *An Index to Changes of Name under the Authority of Acts of Parliament or Royal Licence, 1760-1901* (reprinted 1968)

PINE, L.G., *The Genealogist's Encyclopaedia* (1969)

PINE, L.G., *New Extinct Peerages, 1884-1971* (1972)

PINE, L.G., *Truth in Genealogy: the work of Genealogical Reference Books* (1960 edn.)

PRITCHARD, M.E.L., 'The Genealogy of the Poor' (*Genealogist's Magazine*, vol. 11, no. 3, Sept. 1951)

POLLOCK, E.M., *Manors, their History and their Records* (1933)

POOLE, R.L., *Studies in Chronology and History* (1934)

POWER, D., 'Some early English doctors and their descendants' (*Genealogist's Magazine*, vol. 7, 1935-7)

POWICKE, F.M., and FRYDE, E.B., *Handbook of British Chronology* (Royal Historical Society, 2nd edn., 1961)

Public Record Office List of Plea Rolls of Various Courts (P.R.O. Lists and Indexes, vol. 4, 1910)

PURVIS, J.S., *Dictionary of Ecclesiastical Terms* (1962)

PURVIS, J.S., *Introduction to Ecclesiastical Records* (1953)

PURVIS, J.S., *The Archives of the York Diocesan Registry* (1952)

RADBROOK, W., *Quarter Sessions, Seize Quartiers, etc.* (1909)

RAVEN-HART, H., and JOHNSTON, M., 'Bibliography of the printed registers of the universities, inns of court, colleges and schools of Great Britain and Ireland' (*Bulletin of the Institute of Historical Research*, vol. 9, 1932; vol. 10, 1933)

Record Repositories in Great Britain (Historical Manuscripts Commission, 1966)
Records of the Honourable Society of Lincoln's Inn: part 1, admissions 1420-1893 (2 vols., 1896); part 2, Black Books, 1422-1845 (4 vols., 1897-1902)
REDSTONE, L., and STEER, F.W., *Local Records: their nature and care* (1953)
Return of Owners of Land, 1873 (H.M.S.O., 1875, 2 vols.)
RIDGE, C.H., 'Scientific Genealogy' (*Genealogist's Magazine*, vol. 6, no. 10, June 1934)
ROBISON, NEANNIE, F.J., [?], and BARTLETT, HENRIETTA C., *Genealogical Records, Manuscript Entries of Births, Deaths and Marriages taken from Family Bibles, 1581-1967* (1972)
ROGERS, C.D., *The Family Tree Detective* (1983)
Rolls Series, Government Publication: Sectional List No 24, Record Publication, (H.M.S.O.)
ROUND, J.H., *Family Origins and Other Studies* (1930, reprinted 1971)
ROUND, J.H., *Peerage and Pedigree* (2 vols., 1910, reprinted 1971)
ROUND, J.H., *Studies in Peerage and Family History* (1907, reprinted 1971)
Royal Commission on Local Records: Report (His Majesty's Stationery Office, 1902)
Royal Commission on Public Records: Reports (His Majesty's Stationery Office, 1910-19)
RUVIGNY, MARQUIS OF, *Plantagenet Roll of the Blood Royal* (4 vols., 1905-11)
RYE, W., *Records and Record Searching* (1897)
SCHLEGEL, D.M., *Passengers from Ireland: lists of passengers arriving at American ports, 1811-17* (1980 reprint)
SHEEHAN, M.M., 'A List of 13th-century English Wills' (*Genealogist's Magazine*, vol. 9, March 1961)
SHERWOOD, G.F.T., *Chancery Proceedings* (1908)
SHERWOOD, L., 'The Court Baron' (*Amateur Historian*, vol.12, no. 12, 1956)
SIMS, R., *A Manual for the Genealogist, Topographer, Antiquary and Legal Professor* (1888)
SIMS, R., *Index to Pedigrees and Arms in the Heralds' Visitations* (1892, reprinted 1969)
SKEAT, T.C., (ed.), *Catalogue of Manuscript Collections in the British Museum* (1957)
SKEEL, C., 'Medieval Wills' (*History*, vol. 10, 1926)
SMITH, F., *The Lives and Times of our English Ancestors* (2 vols., 1969, reprinted 1980)
SMITH, FRANK, and GARDNER, DAVID, *Genealogical Research in England and Wales* (3 vols., 1966)
SMITH, FRANK, GARDNER, DAVID, and HARLAND, D., *Genealogical Atlas of England and Wales* (1960)
SMITH, F., *A Genealogical Atlas of Scotland*
SMITH, F., *A Genealogical Gazetteer of England* (1977)
SMITH, F., *A Genealogical Gazetteer of Scotland* (1979)
SMITH, F., GARDNER, D., and HARLAND, D., *A Genealogical Atlas of Ireland* (1964)
SMITH, J.C.C., (ed.), 'Calendar of Lambeth Wills, 1282-1667' (*The Genealogist*, n.s. vols. 34-5, 1918-9)
SMITH, J.C.C., et al., (eds.), 'Index of Wills Proved in the Prerogative Court of Canterbury, 1383-1700' (*British Record Society Index Library*, vols. 10, 11, 18, 25, 43-4, 54, 61, 67, 71, 77, 80, 1893-1960)

SOMERVILLE, ROBERT, *Handlist of Record Publications* (1951)
SQUIBB, G.D., *Founders Kin* (1973)
SQUIBB, G.D., *Visitation Pedigrees and the Genealogist* (1964)
STAMP, A.E., *Methods of Chronology* (Historical Association, 1933)
STEEL, D.J., and HONEYCOMBE, G., *Discovering Your Family History* (1980)
STEPHEN, L., and LEE, S., (eds.), *The Dictionary of National Biography* (23 vols., 1908-13; compact edition of 2 vols., 1975)
STEPHENS, W.B., *Sources for English Local History* (1973, reprinted 1984)
STEPHENSON, MILL, *A List of Monumental Brasses in the British Isles* (1926, reprinted in 2 vols. with appendix by R.H. Griffin, 1938, 1965)
STOREY, R.L., *A Short Introduction to Wills* (1966)
STUART, M., *Scottish Family History* (1930, reprinted 1978)
STURGESS, H.A.C., *Register of Admissions to the Honourable Society of the Middle Temple, 15th century to 1944* (3 vols., 1949)
SUMMERS, PETER, (general ed.), *Hatchments in Britain*: vol. 1, Northamptonshire, Warwickshire, Worcestershire; vol. 2, Norfolk and Suffolk; vol. 3, The Northern Counties; vol. 4, Oxfordshire, Buckinghamshire, Bedfordshire, Berkshire, Wiltshire; vol. 5, Kent, Surrey, Sussex; vol. 6, Essex, Middlesex, Hertfordshire, Cambridgeshire, Huntingdonshire
TATE, W.E., *The Parish Chest* (1946, reprinted 1983)
TEPPER, M., *New World Immigrants: a Consolidation of Ship Passenger Lists from Periodical Literature* (1980)
The Genealogist's Handbook (Society of Genealogists, 1971)
THOMPSON, A. HAMILTON, *Parish History and Records* (Historical Association, 1926)
THOMSON, T.R., *A Catalogue of British Family Histories* (3rd edn. with addenda, 1980)
THOYTS, E.E., *How to read Old Documents* (1893, reprinted 1972, 1980)
TOPHAM, R., 'Index to Chancery Proceedings, 1603-1625' [A-L only] (*Genealogist*, n.s. vols. 4, 6-9, 1889-92)
TURNER, W.F., and COXE, H.O., *Calendar of Charters and Rolls Preserved in the Bodleian Library* (1878)
TURTON, LT.-COL. W.H., *The Plantagenet Ancestry: showing over 7,000 of the ancestors of Elizabeth, wife of Henry VII* (1928, reprinted 1975)
UNETT, JOHN, *Making a Pedigree* (1971)
VENN, J., and VENN, J.A., (eds.), *Alumni Cantabrigiensis 1250-1900* (10 vols., 1922-54)
WAGNER, SIR ANTHONY, *Records and Collections of the College of Arms* (1952, reprinted 1974)
WAGNER, SIR ANTHONY, *English Genealogy* (1983)
WAGNER, SIR ANTHONY, *Heralds and Ancestors* (1979)
WAGNER, SIR ANTHONY, TREMLETT, T.D., and LONDON, H.S., 'Rolls of Arms': 'Henry III: the Matthew Paris Shields, c. 1244-57' ed. T.D. Tremlett; 'Glover's Roll 1253-8 and Walford's Roll c. 1273' ed. H.S. London; 'Additions and Corrections to a Catalogue of English Medieval Rolls of Arms' by A. Wagner (*Harleian Society*, vols. 113-4, 1967)
WAGNER, SIR ANTHONY, *Heralds of England* (1967)
WAGNER, SIR ANTHONY, *Historic Heraldry of Britain* (1973)

WAGNER, SIR ANTHONY, *Pedigree and Progress* (1975)
WAITES, B., 'Memoranda Rolls' (*Amateur Historian*, vol. 5)
WALCOT, M.J., (ed.), *Marriage Indexes: how to find them, how to use them, how to compile them* (2nd edn., 1980)
WALNE, PETER, *English Wills: probate records in England and Wales, with a brief note on Scottish and Irish wills* (1964)
WATSON, G.W., 'Marriage Settlements from Collections in the British Museum and Record Offices' (*Genealogist*, n.s. 33-7, 1917-21)
WEBB, S., and WEBB, B., *History of English Local Government* (1963 reprint) 11 vols., 1, the parish and the county; 2-3, the manor and the borough; 4, statutory authorities for special purposes; 5, the story of the King's highway; 6, English prisons under local government; 7-9, English Poor Law history; 10, English Poor Law policy; 11, the history of liquor licensing in England.
WEST, JOHN, *Town Records* (1983)
WEST, JOHN, *Village Records* (1962, new edn. 1982)
WHALLEY, I., *English Handwriting, 1540-1853* (1970)
WHITE, G.H., 'Notes on Anglo-Norman Genealogy' (*Genealogist's Magazine*, vol. 12, 1945)
WHITE, H.C., 'More Scientific Genealogy' (*Genealogist's Magazine*, vol. 11, no. 5, March 1952)
WHITMORE, J.B., *A Genealogical Guide* (1953)
Who's Who and *Who was Who* (annually and every ten years respectively)
WICKS, A.T., 'School Registers' (*Amateur Historian*, vol. 4, no. 1, Autumn 1958)
WILLIAMS, E., *Early Holborn and the Legal Quarter of London* (2 vols., 1927)
WILLIAMS, E.W., *Know Your Ancestors* (1975)
WILLIAMSON, J.B., *Middle Temple Bench Book* (2nd edn. of A.R. Ingpen's work, 1937)
WILLIS, A.J., 'Winchester Guardianship Records after 1700' (*Genealogist's Magazine*, vol. 14, nos. 7-12, Sept. 1963-Dec. 1964; Vol. 15, no. 1, March 1965)
WILLIS, A.J., *Genealogy for Beginners* (1984 edn.)
'Wills of Masons, 1288-1600' (*Masonic Record*, vol. 16, 1935-6)
WOOD, H.J.T., 'Pedigrees from the *de banco* rolls, temp. Henry VII' (*The Genealogist*, n.s. vols. 22-5, 1906-9)
WRIGHT, A., *Court Hand Restored* (10th edn. edited by C.T. Martin, 1912)
WRIGHT, C.E., *English Vernacular Hands from the 12th to the 15th centuries* (1960)
WRIGHT, JOSEPH, *The English Dialect Dictionary* (1898)
WRIGHT, JOSEPH, *The English Dialect Grammar* (1905)
WROTTESLEY, G., *Pedigrees from the Plea Rolls, 1200-1500* (1905)

2. *JOURNALS*
The Amateur Historian (1952-1968; in 1969 changed title to *The Local Historian*. Journal of the Standing Conference on Local History and later of the British Association for Local History
The Ancestor: a quarterly review of county and family history, heraldry and antiquities (vols. 1-12, 1902-5, edited by Oswald Barron)
Archives (founded 1949)
Archivum (founded 1965)

Bulletin of the Institute of Historical Research (founded 1922)
The Coat of Arms: quarterly journal of the Heraldry Society (founded 1950)
Collectanae Topographica and Genealogica (vols. 1-8, 1834-43)
Economic History Review (founded 1927)
English Historical Review
Family History: journal of the Institute of Heraldic and Genealogical Studies (founded 1962)
Genealogical Journal: journal of the Utah Genealogical Association (founded 1972)
Genealogical Magazine (vols. 1-8, 1897-1904)
Genealogical Queries and Memoranda (vols. 1 and 2, May 1896-May 1900)
The Genealogist (vols. 1-7, n.s. vols 1-38, 1877-1922)
The Genealogist: journal for the promotion of scholarship in genealogical studies (founded 1980)
The Genealogist's Magazine: journal of the Society of Genealogists (founded 1925)
History
History Today (founded 1951)
Journal of Economic History (founded 1941)
Journal of the Society of Archivists (founded 1955)
The Local Historian (see *Amateur Historian* above)
Local Population Studies (founded 1968)
Miscellanea Genealogica et Heraldica (ser. 1-5, 1866-1938)
Topographer and Genealogist (vols. 1-3, 1846-58)

3. GUIDES TO COLLECTIONS OF MANUSCRIPTS AND PRINTED MANUSCRIPTS

Calendar of the Close Rolls preserved in the Public Record Office, from Henry III, 1227 (1902-)
Calendar of the Fine Rolls preserved in the Public Record Office, from Edward I, 1272 (1911-)
Calendar of the Patent Rolls preserved in the Public Record Office, from Henry 111, 1216 (1901-)
Calendar of State Papers Domestic...preserved in the Public Record Office, from Edward VI, 1547 (1856-)
Canterbury and York Society Publications (1907-)
Inquisitiones Post Mortem:
1154-1485: *Calendarium Inquisitionum Post Mortem sive Escaetarum* (Public Record Office, eds. J. Caley and J. Bayley, 4 vols., 1806-28)
1216-1377: *Calendar of Inquisitiones Post Mortem* (14 vols., 1865)
1216-1307: *Calendarium Genealogicum: Henry III and Edward I* (ed. C. Roberts, 2 vols., 1865)
1307-1327: *Calendarium Genealogicum: or Calendar of Heirs...Inquisitiones temp. Edward II* (ed. J.A. Vincent, *The Genealogist*, n.s. vols. 1-4, n.s.6, 1884-7, 1889)
1485-1649: *Indexes to the Inquisitiones Post Mortem* (ed. T. Phillipps, Middle Hill, Typis, Medio-Montanis, 1865)
1509-1649: *Inquisitiones Post Mortem temp. Henry VIII-Charles I* (*The Genealogist*, n.s. vols. 9-19, 1893-1903; 25-34, 1908-20)
1509-1649: *Index of Inquisitiones Post Mortem* (Public Record Office Lists and Indexes nos. 23, 26, 31, 33, 1907-9)

Fasti Ecclesiae Anglicanae (general editor J. Le Neve, 1954-) *Harleian Society Publications* (1869-)

Index Library, British Record Society (1888-)

List of the Records of the Board of Customs and Excise from 1697 at the Public Record Office

Manorial Society Publications include: 'List of Manor Court Rolls in private hands' (3 vols., 1908-13); 'Descriptive catalogue of manorial rolls belonging to Sir H.F. Burke' (2 vols., 1922-3); 'Catalogue of manorial documents at New College, Oxford' (1929); 'List and index of Court Rolls' (with the Public Record Office [?], 1896)

Reports of the Royal Commission on Historical Manuscripts (1874-)

Guide to the Reports of the R.C.H.M. (1914, 1938, 1965)

Reports of the Deputy Keeper of Public Records (1840-1858); continued as the *Annual Report of the Keeper of Public Records and of the Advisory Council on Public Records* (1959-)

Index to the Reports, nos. 1-39 (2 vols., 1865-80)